This book is drawn from discussions that have taken place in the American Theatre Wing Working in the Theatre Seminars series, a fixture in the New York City theatre community for more than three decades. A unique opportunity for theatre artists to engage in sustained conversations about the field, the seminars were begun in the early 1970s, by ATW president Isabelle Stevenson, as panel discussions taking place at theatres around the city, pioneering the idea of allowing audiences to hear directly from artists and administrators about the creation of theatre. Since 1979, ATW has partnered with CUNY TV, the television arm of The City University of New York, to bring these discussions into homes throughout New York City, and beginning in 2003, the seminars have been available to audiences internationally on the Internet via both the ATW and CUNY TV Web sites.

The seminars on which this book is based were hosted or moderated by Theodore Chapin, Thomas Cott, Jim Dale, Jean Dalrymple, Dasha Epstein, Brendan Gill, Sondra Gilman, Henry Hewes, Jeffrey Eric Jenkins, Doug Leeds, Pia Lindström, Lonny Price, Howard Sherman, Isabelle Stevenson, Peter Stone, George C. White, and Edwin Wilson.

Other titles planned from Continuum in the Working in the Theatre series are devoted to Writing, Directing, and Producing and the Theatre Business.

Acting

WORKING IN THE THEATRE

**AMERICAN
THEATRE
WING**
Founder of the Tony Awards®

EDITED BY
Robert Emmet Long

FOREWORD BY
Kate Burton

A GINIGER BOOK

continuum

NEW YORK • LONDON

2006

The Continuum International Publishing Group Inc
80 Maiden Lane, New York NY 10038

The Continuum International Publishing Group Ltd
The Tower Building, 11 York Road, London SE1 7NX

The K. S. Giniger Company Inc
250 West 57 Street, New York NY 10107

www.continuumbooks.com

The Tony Awards are a registered service mark of the American Theatre Wing.

Printed in the United States of America

Library of Congress Cataloging-in-Publication Data

Acting—working in the theatre / edited by Robert Emmet Long.
    p.   cm.—(The American Theatre Wing working in the theatre series ; 1)
  Includes index.
  "A Giniger Book."
  ISBN-13: 978-0-8264-1804-3 (hardcover : alk. paper)
  ISBN-10: 0-8264-1804-X (hardcover : alk. paper)
  ISBN-13: 978-0-8264-1805-0 (pbk. : alk. paper)
  ISBN-10: 0-8264-1805-8 (pbk. : alk. paper)
  1. Theater—United States—Anecdotes.   2. Performing arts—United
States—Anecdotes.   3. Acting—Quotations, maxims, etc.   I. Long, Robert
Emmet. II. Series.
  PN2266.5.A28 2006
  792.0973—dc22

                                                              2006009525

For Isabelle Stevenson,
President and Chairman of
the American Theatre Wing,
from 1966 to 2003,
who got everyone to start talking.

Contents

Foreword by Kate Burton

What a pleasure it is to be asked to write this foreword. I have watched so many of these American Theatre Wing "Working in the Theatre" seminars and participated in two of them. Mostly what I remember is the laughter.

There is nothing that an actor loves talking about more than the things that went wrong, comically and tragically. My father, the great actor Richard Burton, regaled me with stories from early childhood of mishaps on the stage; forgetting his lines, somebody coming on with the wrong prop or no prop at all, awful things that were said to him about his performance. But through all the mishaps, what was shining through was "the moment"; the moment you first walked onstage, said your first line, learned you had the part, walked into the audition.

My most important "moment" watching my Dad was the first time he performed in *Equus* on Broadway. I had not seen him onstage since I was very tiny. He went on for his first performance unexpectedly, so as not to have an overly hysterical audience. The stage manager, Bob Borod, said over the PA, "Ladies and Gentlemen, at this performance the role of Dr. Dysart usually played by Anthony Perkins will be played by Richard Burton."

The audience went wild. The play began. The brilliantly conceived "horses" are in their stalls. The boy, Alan Strang, nuzzles one of them. My father stands up. He speaks: "With a horse called Nugget, he embraces." My father's voice, his presence—you could have heard a pin drop. The hair stood up on the back of my neck. I understood what it was that made my Dad so thrilling to watch. It was his ability to take the "moment." I was twenty.

What you will hear in these pages are a lot of "moments" of some of the greatest actors and actresses of the English–speaking stage. Every actor has a few of these but they are memorable to them. I had two that I remember as seismic. They were in two of the most perfect plays that have ever been written: *The Beauty Queen of Leenane* by Martin McDonagh and *Hedda Gabler* by Henrik Ibsen.

I took over the role of Maureen from the Tony Award–winner Marie Mullen. The play is gritty and merciless but wildly funny. I had a monologue in the second act that was very dreamy and poetic, unlike anything else in the play. I found it very difficult to do because at the end of it I had to wield a fireplace poker as I was to hit someone with it. Garry Hynes (the first female director to win the Tony!) said that I just needed to let it happen, no forethought, as if it were a natural thing. It seemed weird but I tried it . . . and it worked. She said, "You see, Kate, it is at this moment that the play becomes a 'theatre machine.'" The story turns on its axis. The audience is sucked into the vortex of the character's mind. I felt that "moment" every time I did it from Broadway to Belfast to Brighton.

Years later, I would feel it again playing Hedda Gabler. A much quieter moment. It is a few moments after Eilert Lovbörg arrives. He has been talked about for a long time. Hedda is onstage with Judge Brack and her husband, George Tesman. Eilert arrives, they all talk although Hedda says very little, she watches and listens, and is consumed with Eilert but she cannot express it. Finally, Tesman and Brack leave her alone with Eilert. They look at each other for the first time as who they are, not appendages of other people. The director, Nicholas Martin, had us take a long, long, long look—almost too long, but every time we did it there was electricity between us and it was almost frightening. Hedda and Eilert. The Moment. It is a quiet moment but it is as if a brass band were playing or a symphony, and the play takes off from it. That moment was felt from Bay Street in Sag Harbor to Williamstown to the Huntington in Boston to Broadway. It was one of the keys to the play for me.

These are some of my experiences and now you are about to read about many other experiences. Funny, thrilling, scary, seemingly normal, original. These are culled from many conversations between actors talking about the thing they love the most: acting in the theatre. Enjoy.

Introduction

This volume on acting in the theatre grew out of the enthusiastic response of viewers to the American Theatre Wing seminars on the profession of theatre today. The series is called Working in the Theatre for good reason. The participants, performing throughout North America and the United Kingdom, have devoted their lives to the theatre and can speak about this experience as insiders.

Of all who make up the theatrical community, actors have the most immediate relation to us. A personal relationship is struck as soon as the actor appears onstage. He or she could be any one of us who has imagined himself or herself on the stage.

In these pages, the reader has the opportunity to hear his or her favorites speak—as they are personally. Inevitably, surprises occur as the actors admit to being more vulnerable than might be imagined, or to their holding opinions contrary to what one would have firmly supposed. It is a pleasure to hear them reflect on their respective careers, on what sets them apart in the charmed space they occupy, on what connects them to audiences.

The conversations from which this book is created are free-flowing and unrehearsed. A host or moderator keeps each seminar on track with specific questions and issues—the actor's relationship to his or her audience; differences in training and acting styles in Britain and America; different approaches and techniques in "becoming other people"; the pitfalls for auditioning for a stage role; the problem of staying fresh during the lengthy run of a Broadway or off-Broadway show; the sudden paralyzing onset of fear onstage that can reduce an actor to raw helplessness; the complicated relationship of the actor to the director and playwright; the technical and practical differences in acting for the movies or television and the theatre; the mysterious relationship between actor and audience.

The performers and their backgrounds are almost unimaginably diverse. Some of the actors are the adult children of famous performers, whereas others found their way into the theatre barely having considered becoming an actor in their wildest dreams. They tell of their beginnings—of their appearances in college productions or of training at acting studios; of their apprenticeships in summer stock and regional theatre; and, especially if they are English, of their years performing Shakespeare in repertory. Comical stories are related, involving auditions, the interrelationships among other professionals, the interactions with audiences. Some of the most memorable portions are found in the stories of beginnings or "First Inspirations." One famous actress tells of the report from her acting teacher in England who commented, "At this time, we see no sign of talent."

A few words about the structure of the volume and the process of turning fleeting conversation into the permanence of a book are in order. It has been organized to bring together and place into high relief recurring themes from three decades of broadcast transcripts, and in so doing to create a compact and dynamic volume consisting of as many voices as possible. Often, comparable or contrasting views are arranged for maximum effect. Synthesizing many thousands of pages of conversation, literally from different eras, into one modest-sized volume to showcase the range of American Theatre Wing seminars has been quite a challenge. Some of the excerpts have been lightly edited to provide maximum fluency in the conversations. Basic biographical sketches and an index are included for easy reference.

In perusing these pages, the reader will immediately be conscious of the camaraderie of the actors who come to think of the stage as their home and of the company as their family. Although the book is always informative, what drives it is the performers' passion for the theatre—their sense of selfless devotion to their art, regardless of the uncertainties, anxieties, obstacles, and difficulties of an actor's life. Each could have chosen a career more steady, more commonplace; but these remarkable people opted instead for a life that is bold and imaginative. In this respect, we can surely admire every one of them.

ROBERT EMMET LONG

First Inspirations

Rosemary Harris

I wanted to act but I didn't want to be an actress, because I thought that actresses were flighty and inconsequential people, and that I really ought to do something more with my life.

Cherry Jones

I think I was headed in the acting direction my whole life. I did a little tap-dance recital when I was five and it was the end of my dancing career, but I remember the applause and all of that. Then I had a wonderful creative dramatics teacher, Miss Ruby Krider, in my hometown. She always moved me.

I saw Colleen Dewhurst and Jason Robards in *A Moon for the Misbegotten* when I was sixteen and in a summer program at Northwestern University, which was incredibly influential.

Then, I went to Carnegie Mellon and that was very influential. But I think probably what led me here was coming to New York, and getting into the Brooklyn Academy of Music Theatre Company, which I was really lousy in. I was twenty-three and I didn't have an idea in the world what I was doing. But a crazy Rumanian director named Andrei Belgrader saw me in the show I was doing, and cast me as Rosalind in *As You Like It* and took me up to the American Repertory Theatre in Cambridge, Massachusetts, where I did rep for six out of ten seasons. And that's where I grew up as an actor.

Finally, at I think the age of thirty-three, I felt I could hang out my shingle as an actor since I finally had the experience I needed. I guess it was getting the part of Rosalind and going to that rep company that was the fork in my road. I don't know that I would have survived as an actor if I hadn't had a home where I could be nourished.

Patrick Stewart

For me, there were three separate forks. The first one was at twelve with my English master. And you know, at least in the classical theatre in England, there's invariably an English teacher lurking somewhere in all actors' backgrounds. He cast me in a play. And the first time I walked onstage, I knew that I was in the safest place that I'd ever been. Life wasn't too safe for me when I was growing up. The stage was absolutely home.

And then at fifteen, I left school. Not because I dropped out, as the rumor got around. I didn't drop out. I had finished the minimum that the State required then in England. I was working on a local newspaper and doing a lot of amateur acting, and this conflicted with my duties as a newspaper reporter. The editor gave me an ultimatum, which was to give up all my amateur acting and become a reporter, or leave his newspaper. I packed up my typewriter within half-an-hour and I was out of the building, with my friend hanging on my heels, saying, "You're making a terrible mistake! Don't do this!" I tried to find out how to become an actor.

Roscoe Lee Browne

What a pity, I have a feeling I've had a misspent life, when I realize that everybody started so early. Well, of course, there was no television when I was young. There was hardly a crystal set. In 1956, I was already well in my thirties, and I was working for Schenley Import Corporation as something called a national-sales representative. I had the position because I was a runner, as they say, I ran track. I think I was about the first of those world-class athletes that is given a job because he is an athlete, and mainly to represent liquor companies.

I worked for them for four years, and the end of the fourth year, 1956, the import company and the domestic company merged. The president called me down and said, "Well, kid, we're merging. I thought we'd tell you, all you guys, before it hit the papers on Monday. But we have a great, marvelous new job for you. It's for an exec and it's great." I said, "I have to think about that and will call you on Monday."

I made dinner that night and invited three friends. Three extraordinary ladies, and they came. One of them asked finally, "What do you want to tell us, darling?" It was Josephine Premice, and she always said "darling." And I blurted out: "I was just thinking tomorrow I'm going to become an actor."

I thought they would kill me, but Jo went out and bought three trade papers: *Variety, Show Business,* and I think it was *Back Stage.* She got them to prove to me that acting would be the most unlikely thing for me to do. She would say, "Now, here's a role and there'll be twenty-thousand actors up for that one. You're black and you're not a kid."

I saw on page twenty five in one of the magazines that the following day would be the last for actors to audition for the inaugural season of the NY Shakespeare Festival. So, I went downtown to that little church on the Lower East Side. I didn't presumably think I could act, but I knew at least I had read the literature. That was why they hired me, because I seemed to speak it and understand it. That's how I became an actor.

Jennifer Ehle

I've done everything in reverse, I think, because the only reason I do it is I've got some chromosome glitch where I really do passionately want to be someone else and don't have a very strong sense of self in some ways. I always wanted to do anything I could to be somebody else, but I was always too shy ever to stand up in front of anybody and do it.

It wasn't until after I first started being in front of a camera, and after I had left drama school, that I began to really feel that nobody was watching me when I was doing it and that I could actually go through the wardrobe. And the last two years is only when I've begun to feel that onstage. So, as I say, I've sort of done it all in reverse. And now I'm passionate about it.

Kate Burton

I came from an acting family. So, I think I probably started acting when I was about one or one-and-a-half. Actually, I did step onto the stage doing a performance of *Camelot*, in 1961 apparently, at the age of four. It was the moment when Arthur realizes that something's going on between Lancelot and Guinevere. And I was sitting on the lap of the dresser and saw my Dad get very choked up. And I thought, *What's wrong? I must comfort him.* So, I walked onto the stage to do that.

Heather Headley

My first introduction to the musical theatre was in the Caribbean. Living in the Caribbean, we have a lot of imports of Indian film and music. There is a lot of dancing and singing. So, I just thought that's how all American films were. When I saw my first movie, which was *The Sound of Music*, I just thought, *That's what they do!* And so that's what I did,

I sang. And when we got to the States, they introduced me to musicals, and that was it. I just fell in love after that.

Hallie Foote

I began late. My father is a writer [Horton Foote], and I've been around the business, in a way, all my life. He was always determined to keep us as far away from it as possible. I went to college, I got married . . . I was sort of floundering. And one day, I decided I wanted to try acting. I guess I was about twenty three or twenty four—it was late for most people I guess—when I said to my father, "I think I'd like to try acting."

There was this pause: I think he thought he had escaped having to deal with that. He finally said, "Well, if you want to do this, you ought to study with somebody." I ended up going to Los Angeles and studying with a woman named Peggy Feury and a man named William Traylor. I studied for about three, four years, and then I came to New York and started working. Actually, I did a play of my Dad's. He brought me here.

Gregory Hines

I started as a tap dancer when I was two-and-a-half. My brother was four at the time, and our parents gave us tap lessons. They felt that this would be a way to give us something. At the time, the occupations for most black people were either in the post office or sports

Tom Hulce

I decided I wanted to be an actor when I was fifteen. I wanted to be a singer but my voice changed and I was impatient. I went away for a year to a school in Michigan, where I grew up, called the Interlochen Arts Academy. And then went to North Carolina School of the Arts. I was in a big hurry to come to New York to try and work.

One thing that I did then, I think it was the best decision I made, was every summer I would go someplace where I thought they were doing work that was the best I could be in close proximity to. So, I wasn't going someplace where I could play good parts but where I could be just a part of good work.

Tyne Daly

I was born into the family business. Two out of the four of us siblings went into it as a profession. I love stories. I was read a lot of stories as a kid. I like being a storyteller. I went around to find people that knew more about it. I went to college for a year at Brandeis because Jasper Deeter was there, who ran the Hedgerow Theatre. He was an amazing teacher. He taught me stagecraft, how to make a stage manager's book, lighting, props, everything.

After he left, they weren't going to let me act—I was also in a hurry—until I was a junior, which seemed forever! So, I flunked out of German and came to work with Philip Burton who had a wonderful school, and went for formal training for two years there, the theory being that if you are going to be an American actor, you also have to be able to move and to sing.

It was the American Music and Dramatic Academy, fashioned, I guess, a little bit after LAMDA [London Academy of Music and Dramatic Arts]. I started to work. The luck of the work took us away to New York, and I thought I was leaving the theatre forever, and got to the Coast and found out there was a lot of active stuff going on, and did a play a year or better out there, sometimes for free, in waiver houses and at the Los Angeles Actor's Theatre.

Kathleen Chalfant

I acted when I was a kid in high school. I grew up in Oakland and I was in a theatre group there, taken there by somebody, and my father used to come and take me away at midnight, saying that I'd been a slave. Then, I went to college, thinking that I was going to study theatre and I didn't. I studied classical Greek instead.

I was on my way to getting a master's degree in classical Greek and I met my husband and said to him, "You know, I really don't want to teach Greek in a prep school." And he asked, "What do you want to do?" And I said, "Well, I always wanted to be an actor." "Well, why don't you do that?" And so, I did. I began in a strange way.

I didn't ever go to acting school. We were married and I went to Europe and I studied in Europe with someone. And then we came back and moved to New York when I was twenty-eight, and I began to study with Wynn Handman.

And I worked in the theatre for twenty-six years, doing mostly new plays and being incredibly lucky in the writers with whom I've worked. My first big thing was Jules Feiffer's *Hold Me*, then *Sister Mary [Ignatius Explains It All to You]*. So, I've made my way slowly and I've been lucky since I've had the luxury of staying in New York and doing what I like.

Matthew Broderick

My debut was in *Torch Song Trilogy*, when I was nineteen. Before that? My father was James Broderick, an actor, who I grew up watching onstage, all over the country. I spent a lot of summers at various theatres, summer-stock places, and watched him. I guess that's where I started wanting to be an actor, although I didn't really admit that for years until I was in my late teens in high school. Then I started. Really.

Where I learned most of my acting-school-type stuff was in high school, believe it or not, which gets a bad reputation sometimes. This was Walden, which doesn't exist anymore. But I did three plays a year and I learned a lot.

After that, I studied with Uta Hagen a little bit and then I was lucky enough to get the job when I was nineteen in *Torch Song Trilogy*, with Harvey Fierstein, which is a great way to begin because you've seen everything.

That led to *Brighton Beach Memoirs*. I was so excited that day, mostly by the play. I thought *Brighton* was such a fantastically good part and a wonderful play. And it was by Neil Simon, who I thought really was a factory that made shows. I didn't know "it" was a guy until that day.

Elizabeth Franz

I always wanted to be an actor, since I was five-years old. It was either a missionary or an actress. My mother wanted me to be a missionary. I feel it's almost the same thing.

I read in *Seventeen* magazine, back in Akron, Ohio, about the American Academy of Dramatic Arts, and I went there at nineteen. I left Ohio and came to New York, to the American Academy.

Lonette McKee

My mother began taking me around to all the nightclubs in Detroit. I would go onstage and tell the band what to play—even though I never studied music. I didn't know what key or anything to tell them. I would just sit at the piano and say, "OK, play it like this."

I would do this little act, with my mother as chaperone. And when I was around fourteen, I got my first hit record in Detroit. Then, I left Detroit and went to L.A. You would think I'd come to New York, to do theatre, from Detroit. But I didn't know about that.

Alan Alda

My father did not want me to be an actor. He was an actor. He wanted me to be a doctor because that's what he always wanted to be. Nevertheless, he brought me onstage when I was six-months old. He was working in burlesque and he brought me, as a joke, to the other actors. And I was onstage with him for various times throughout my childhood—he still tried to talk me out of becoming an actor. And I did the same thing with my children. I tried to talk them out of becoming actresses, but then I wrote parts for them in movies. It's a genetic quirk in my family.

Jerry Orbach

I had a very strange mixture of singing and acting [in my background]. I sang in little clubs and at high-school dances. By accident, I ended up in the Illinois State singing contest and won. I sang "Without a Song"—actually, it was leather-lung yelling rather than singing. In college, I was a serious dramatic actor. Musicals were alien to me. I looked down on them. But when I came to New York, I found that this was the way I could earn my living. Being able to sing narrowed the competition. Friends who could act but not sing ended up going to California to find work. I was able to stay in New York and work by singing.

Michael Crawford

I actually started with opera. I started with Benjamin Britten. When I was about twelve, thirteen, fourteen, I was singing in *Let's Make an Opera* and *Noah's Flood*. I failed for *Turn of the Screw*, but I was very close to opera from an early age.

People say, "We were surprised by your casting in *Phantom of the Opera.*" I can actually say, "Well no, I don't think you should be, since thirty-two years ago I was in opera."

Brian Dennehy

I went to Columbia but I didn't do any acting there. I played football at Columbia and then I was in the Marine Corps for five years, during this "disturbance" in Southeast Asia. By that time, I had a wife and two kids with one on the way. My father expected me to go to law school or graduate school. For some unaccountable reason, I said, "No, I want to be an actor!"

Well, for an Irish working-class family in Brooklyn, especially when you have two kids, this was kind of an unusual announcement to make. I have no idea what brought me that feeling. I had done some acting in high school, had a wonderful high-school teacher. We probably all can mention some person who changed our lives. This person's name was Chris Sweeney, and he was a tough, working-class guy. There are these wonderful Irishmen who are self-made intellectuals. He was a reader, a thinker, and a philosopher. He got me started acting in this high school in Brooklyn, this very tough, Catholic high school, all boys, jackets and ties.

In those days, there wasn't a ban on corporal punishment. They'd whack you just as soon as look at you. Anyway, I did *Macbeth* at fourteen in front of this very tough audience. People say, "Boy, that was a really, really brave thing to do." And I say, "That was brave? You should have seen the poor kid who played Lady Macbeth!"

That's how it all started. But then I got away from it for ten years. When I came back from the service—you mature quickly—you have to. You really get to the end asking, *What do I want to do with my life?* Because this is a precious piece of time. And this is what I decided to do. Ten years of driving cabs and driving trucks and working in bars, and I was "an overnight success."

Donna Murphy

What was hard for me about New York University was that, since I hadn't grown up in the New York area, I found the distraction of the business really hard. I was taking my academics at the university and studying at the conservatory, Stella Adler's class.

I was really star struck and started buying *Back Stage* and *Show Business* and going to open calls, and got to a Broadway show. I went to an open call for a musical and I got a job, my sophomore year in college.

I found that I wasn't really mature enough to stay focused in class. And then, I went back later, not to NYU but to class with a different teacher and studied some more.

The great thing about being at NYU is the very thing that distracted me. New York is an incredible city. The museums, the people-watching, the libraries, just the city itself and the energy of it are phenomenal. And the people who teach there are the best.

Lucie Arnaz

Acting is something I wanted to do from a very early age. Most people work doing a little play here and there and whatnot and try to get a television series one day. I started on a television series that was in the top ten for six years, and I learned a lot of good things since we worked with a lot of famous people. Every week, they had a guest star, everyone from Wally Cox to Carol Burnett to the Burtons.

You can certainly learn from watching other people do what they do, right or wrong.

Kate Burton

I had no intention of being an actress because I didn't want to follow in the family tradition. I graduated with a degree in history and Russian studies, determined to be a diplomat, which has served me in good stead. Then I thought, *Oh, no, I better give it a shot,* and went to the Yale School of Drama for three years, much to my Dad's chagrin. He wanted me to go to RADA [Royal Academy of Dramatic Arts] or LAMDA. And I said, "No, I'm an American."

Jessica Lange

I was in some remote little town in northern Minnesota, in junior-high school, and we had to—as an assignment—do a monologue for speech class. I had never thought about the theatre. I had no exposure to culture of any kind up there in the woods. I didn't even know where to look.

They handed out mimeographed copies of different monologues to all the students and said, "Pick one." And the very first one I read, I thought, "OK, well—wow! This is something. I'll do this one" And it was "the jonquil speech" from *The Glass Menagerie.* I've come full circle, forty years later. Now, I'm actually playing the character.

Jefferson Mays

At the end of every meal, we would read a family novel. We would read *David Copperfield* or *Great Expectations,* generally Dickens, some Thurber. All five of us would pass the novel around the table and each read a few pages or a chapter. And I think that was the first time that I encountered theatre. It was just the spoken word and these wonderful narratives, and hearing my father's voice—he was sort of a removed narrator. My mother would inhabit every character very fully, and I remember watching her face just transform as she was reading.

I was very frustrated with those Dickensian sentences that go on for pages and coming to all those commas, and I would just be furious. And in my preliterate days—well, I couldn't read of course in my preliterate days—so, I would hear a Mr. Monroe story from James Thurber and then I would get up and sort of act out a little Mr. Monroe vignette of some kind. I think that was my introduction to theatre. It was just sort of around the campfire of the dining-room table.

Lynn Redgrave

I was determined that, once I decided I was going to act, it was my idea. I became totally stage struck and I tried to convince myself that it was my idea. I remember the first dramatic school I auditioned for was the London Academy of Music and Dramatic Art. I had all this wonderful coaching I could have had at home on my pieces, but I didn't want to do anything with them. I was also terminally shy, so I didn't know how to ask anyone at home to hear my speeches or to give me coaching. I asked an actor friend for some advice and was told "to take my moment." I thought that was good advice. At the audition, they told me "at your own time." So, I turned and faced the back wall. I didn't know what to do when I was facing the back wall. I didn't know anything about preparing a role. Nothing. When I had done that long enough, I turned around and did a piece from *The Two Gentleman of Verona* and a bit of Jean Anouilh's *The Lark*. The letter came back, "At this time, we see no sign of talent."

Martha Plimpton

My mother [Shelley Plimpton] was in the original company of *Hair* at the Public Theater in 1967. And she then moved to Broadway with it in 1968. And my father [Keith Carradine] came in to replace James Rado as Claude, and that was in 1970. I was conceived in the spring of that year. I'm not sure if it was in the Biltmore Theatre or somewhere around it. There was a lot going on!

By the end of 1970, when I emerged, wet and screaming from my mother's womb, I was in the theatre every single day until I was about three-years old. And my babysitters were "The Tribe," these wonderful, wonderful actors. These were strange people who just had literally pulled out of Washington Square Park to be in the show. These people cared for me and raised me.

I didn't know any other life, which at times has frustrated me since I've often felt, *Well, you know, maybe I would be a better actor had I come to it as a young woman rather than as an infant.* Had I made a conscious decision, maybe I would approach it differently, be more intellectual about it; have a more rigorous technique or system if I had gone to college or what have you.

But I didn't. I just grew up in it, and spent most of my life going to plays and seeing pretty much everything. My mother had no restrictions on what I was permitted to see, from a very early age. I remember seeing a production of *Titus Andronicus* that just blew my five-year-old brain.

Michel Bell

There were seven of us at home and my Mom and Dad. It was a lot of fun because we used to embarrass my Mom by going out in the neighborhood and just performing right on the corner, no matter what it was.

This is Fresno, California. Right on the corner. And she would be so embarrassed that she would sneak out of the house behind one of the bushes. "Come here! I said, *come here!*" And we're just oblivious, singing, "La cucaracha" or whatever it is. Seven of us, lined up in a chain.

The funny thing is, people would drive by and slow down, and look and some would stop, watch, and start laughing then applauding.

Out of the seven of us, I'm the only one who kind of took it seriously. [It takes,] I don't know whether it's a vivid imagination or just the innate ability to internalize something that you really, really want. You turn it around and you become what that is. It's something that's hard to explain. But the whole point is to take that and be in your own little world, and have that become reality within yourself.

Rob Marshall

I was too mortified to go to dance class, so [my sister] Kathleen [Marshall] actually used to teach me in the basement of our house. It was just too weird for a guy to go do dance class. I just couldn't. The whole dance-belt thing was really frightening—that whole world.

Joel Grey

I had no musical training. I had some tap lessons when I was about eleven and I hated it. I actually wanted to be a ballet dancer, but I couldn't take the guff. I couldn't take the kids at school making fun of me, because that was really my passion.

Vanessa Redgrave

It was in the war and we were evacuated. And there was a boy who was four years older than my brother or me. I suppose I was about four-and-a-half. And his father and mother had given him the materials to make himself a theatre. He'd got electric lights and he made it himself, with their help, with money and so on. And he invented plays. He did all the voices. Bit by bit, he grudgingly admitted that maybe my brother and I might be helping in some sort of way.

Then he started to write plays with living actors, instead of models with plaster scenery that you move on the end of sticks across the stage. So, he started writing plays and we performed them. The audience paid a half-penny, which used to go to the merchant seamen's fund for distressed families in the war. And so it was moments of illusion—that's why I went into the theatre.

Rick Lyon

My story is typical of many, many puppeteers of my generation. The first puppetry that I saw was on TV, *Kukla, Fran & Ollie,* Burr Tillstrom and his wonderful work. And [there were] other children's shows like *Captain Kangaroo*—Mr. Moose was one of the first puppets I ever saw on TV. And it was something that immediately fascinated me.

The first live puppet show I ever saw was at the 1964 World's Fair. Despite the fact that it was not great theatre, it was still unbelievably exciting to me because it was live. That was the first time I'd seen a puppet live and that was a life-changing event. I don't know, where do proclivities for human existence come from? I don't know. It was something that always attracted me, right away.

I think one of the reasons it attracted me was, once I found out more about it and started studying—*Well, who are these people? How do they do that?*—[I realized] it encompasses an incredibly broad range of artistic disciplines. The average puppeteer is creating his own material and designing his puppets and creating his puppets, painting the scenery, making the set, and ultimately performing as well.

Phylicia Rashad

Well, beauty was always an issue for me as a child because my parents were absolutely stunning. My sister was cute as pie. All of the girls ran after my brother. But every time I looked in the mirror, I thought, *Well, when I was born, God was on a lunch break.* This is how young people can think. It's really something when you're always comparing yourself to people around you. If you're always comparing yourself to other people, you can trick yourself easily into believing you're greater than or less than, instead of just being who you are.

When I was eleven-years old, because of my speech patterns, I was selected to be the mistress of ceremonies for an interscholastic musical presentation, with all of the schools. I had learned my script so well, and on the night of the performance I stood in the spotlight for the first time. The light was blinding. I had my script in my hand. But because

I had studied it and prepared so well, I didn't have to read it. I stood there and talked to the light, and I just talked to the light all night long.

And when the evening was finished and people were leaving, I heard several mothers say, "Oh, there's the little girl who spoke so beautifully! Isn't she beautiful?!" And I thought, *That's it! When I grow up, I'll be an actress and be beautiful all the time.* But what I didn't understand, and wouldn't be able to articulate for many years, was that the beauty that I had experienced had nothing to do with what I was wearing or the curls in my hair, or the ruffles on my socks. It was the beauty of communication from the heart. That's what acting is.

Anne Heche

It's funny, I feel my pretending happened very young. We were not only pretending we weren't from the place we were from, which was rural Ohio, we were pretending that we were not the people that we were. We were pretending that we were richer than we were. We were pretending we were not living in the house that we were living in. This was not our car. These were not our clothes. The whole thing was a big fat pretend. So, I do feel that I was learning from a very, very young age to lie very well.

2

Training, Technique, Preparation

Elizabeth Franz

The beautiful thing that happened to me was all of my training came from a wonderful couple that ran one of those—they're almost all gone—summer theatres, where you can go and you can do sixteen plays in sixteen weeks. And you do everything in that—stage managing, the lights—you learn theatre. You learn how to create characters, and get up there and do it. I spent about four years with them, in my early twenties.

Swoosie Kurtz

I worked for years in regional theatre, just all over the place, Manitoba, Cincinnati, the Charles Playhouse in Boston, the Arena Stage, the Goodman, just everywhere. I finally got a show in New York, *The Effect of Gamma Rays on Man-in-the-Moon Marigolds,* in which I was playing a nice, little cameo, understudying the two girls and then I got to play both parts. They both left rather quickly and I played both of them for the next two years.

Dana Ivey

I avoided New York. I was very frightened of New York and I stayed in the regions. I actually went to Canada and worked up there for eight years because I loved English theatre so much and I knew that, at that time particularly, English theatre was more available up there than in the U.S. So, I went there and worked all across Canada for eight years. I did a season in Winnipeg, two in Calgary, two in Montreal. And [to] every young person—I wouldn't trade anything in the world for that experience, but I'm glad I did it when I was young.

Patrick Stewart

Someone once defined to me craft—or technique as I've always thought of it—as being what you use when you don't feel it anymore.

Diahann Carroll

My first important teacher was Lee Strasberg. I studied with him for a long period of time. He was the first person I ever worked with—the first male—who gave me direct criticism. I found that I needed that. I needed someone to jolt me in that way, it was very important to me. He would also make me explain my selections—the strange properties I chose— and then how I prepared to play, very often, a white girl in a part. What it was that made me gravitate toward this role.

Richard Easton

I never had any acting classes, as such, since there wasn't any such thing when I started. But I took ballet class and I took fending lessons, and I took singing lessons and voice and elocution, and walking around with books on my head and all that. "How now, brown cow?" and all that stuff. And really never acting classes other than just acting.

Nathan Lane

I have taken some classes. At some point, somebody said to me, "Well, you know, you should study. You should do something, get some sort of foundation." And I took kind of a crash summer course at the Stella Adler Studio.

I didn't work with Stella Adler. That was real smart. I was working with her cousin or something. I was very young and it was a little too abstract for me. She would say, "Go to the window and tell me what you see—you know, de-scribe." And people would go, "Oh, I see a homeless person and I see the poverty of the world. I see dark clouds, and I see the tragedy of life." She asked, "What do you see?"

And I said, "I see four-hundred dollars going down the drain."

Michael Learned

I went to school in England actually, to a vocational school in England. So, it was very structured. It was primarily a ballet school, but we had dance classes every day, different kinds. And I was a special drama student because I was a terrible dancer. They said, "We think maybe you ought to try drama here." But it was fabulous. I was eleven-years-old and we were studying Shakespeare voice production and intercostal diaphragmatic breathing, mime, scenes, and at eleven one's whole physical body was actually being formed, to the point where, by the time you're ready to work, you're forgetting about all the technique. It's just there. It's part of you.

Dana Ivey

Acting is only something that can be done through the training of experience, just as any draftsman may have a gift but he teaches himself by doing it over and over and over. He can't just do it, first time out. You have to be able to do it over and over and over again.

Acting schools are great, but that's not the same as having to go out and deliver to an audience, and communicate with them. And there are not many avenues for young people to do that, I don't think, today.

Lucie Arnaz

It clearly helps to be around people who love to do what you want to do, and do it well. You watch a great shoemaker make a good pair of shoes, you could learn from the best. If it bores you to make shoes, you won't learn no matter what.

Maximilian Schell

Live as fully as you can because the more you stretch out your soul or your heart, the more characters you can portray.

Lily Tomlin

In the beginning I couldn't study very well. I didn't understand, just as I didn't understand how to audition. I would try to incorporate what I'd been learning in class. I'd finish doing a scene, and the kids would look at me as if I were really wacky. It was like, *What was I thinking? What was I doing?* And the teacher would be dumbfounded, too. So, then I stopped. I clearly could not develop technique at that point. I just had to go intuitively.

Swoosie Kurtz

For some reason, it was my dream to go to an English drama school. I was a real Anglophile. I got accepted to the London Academy of Music and Dramatic Art, and went there for two years and came back. I look back now and I think I would have been better off, I would have gone further faster, had I gone to Juilliard or Yale. I would have had a network. I would have known people. Came back, wonderful training, but I came back cold. Nobody knew me. I knew nobody.

Blythe Danner

In London, [there are] the transitions between all of the dramas and comedy and repertory. We don't seem to have all that luxury. We seem to be much more more oriented to success. And if you're doing well you don't dare to sort of disappear to go do something that other people won't see. The flexibility is wonderful that the British people have.

Vanessa Redgrave

I came to New York and saw theatre in New York, not anywhere else, for the first time in 1955. I saw a season with Paul Muni and Frederic March and Shirley Booth and Julie Harris, and at least another ten other of the greats.

Predominantly, there was new work. It was that that made me realize that theatre wasn't, and must not be, what the theatre that I'd seen in England had made me think it should be and must be. I had an idea from British theatre, and I had loved that idea, until I saw American theatre and American actors.

I'd thought theatre is a jewel and it's velvet and it's trumpet fanfares and it is Stratford-on-Avon. It is putting on masses of make-up and having lovely disguises. Sometimes you wear a lovely dress. And one day, you'll stand in the center of the stage and you'll do Portia's casket scene.

That was my idea of theatre until I came in the 1955–56 season that winter. It amazes me to think that that extraordinary talent and life that there was, why anybody would ever want to come to England to study drama. Because, honestly, I can't think that we then had anything to teach them, except some wonderful actors whom you can see.

Adam Pascal

For me, the longer I do a show the more layers of clothing I am able to take off. My intention is to be able to take them all off at once, but I can't do that. I'm just not capable of doing that. I need the experience of an extended run. I need years and years. I need lots of performances and lots of work to be able to take those layers off. It's just about the continual process of doing it night after night, and being able to expose myself just a little bit more and making that performance just a little bit "realer," bringing this character a little bit more to life and making him less like me and more like himself.

Tonya Pinkins

I think of acting more as living truthfully in imaginary circumstances. So, I don't try to get rid of "Tonya." I might try to make Tonya more than Tonya is in her own life, in the process of creating a character. But I begin the work by looking at a script and imagining it as I would want the greatest actor of all time to do it. Then, over the course of rehearsals, taking chances, risking, falling on my face, and trying to get myself to places that maybe I couldn't in my life at all. But if the character has to do that, then I have to do that. In that sense, I don't think I negate myself. I actually expand myself through the work that I do.

Patrick Stewart

I started out believing that acting was a form of disguise and I spent years, decades, elaborately concealing myself. And it took me years to discover that didn't work for me. It was not allowing me a voice to speak. My voice was concealed. Something happened and I changed all of that and now it comes right down to the selection of the work. I look now for work that resonates for me. Not necessarily for great roles or great plays, but something that is pertinent to my life now. And then I put that into the work, and putting myself into the work has become almost the whole process now.

George Rose

For me, speech and character are one and the same. It is the human voice that reaches the top point of the theatre— the very back of the mezzanine. You cannot see facial expressions, you cannot see tears, but the quality and the coloration of the speech—the product of the writer's intentions—is to me the first job of the actor to master. The actor's first job is to be audible to every part of the house.

Ian McKellen

As far as we can make out, Shakespeare's dialect of four-hundred years ago was closer to that of a Southern American than a Southern Englishman. American actors trying to do Shakespeare with British accents are ridiculous and contradicted by that probable fact. I wish that American actors would do it in their own accents.

Jennifer Ehle

I don't think any of us really learned much at all at drama school. I don't know whether that's the fault of the school or not. And I'm not going to say here, since we are being televised, that it is. I just think we were at a school that was going through a strange time.

I'm sure I have some craft. I survived fifteen months at the Royal Shakespeare Company. I didn't think I would but I did, so it must be that. But I think it's come from doing things. It shifts from part to part. The part teaches you and the play teaches you.

Jean Smart

I wish that more theatre schools would have a class on the realities of the business. And I don't mean just every once in a while bringing in a professional actor to talk about his or her career, because that usually ends up with them telling theatre stories or stories about parts that they did, which is great, too. Not just about auditioning and meeting agents. I'm talking about what you do when you're an actor and you're married, and you have children.

Maxwell Caulfield

In England, it is much easier to find an actor who can play an American man of means, but if they have to play some kid from the Bronx, it's usually very hard. They have to bring the American actor over to do it. Most actors are mimics and it should be pretty easy to pick up other voices and dialects. If you speak all the time in your own voice, it's boring.

Adam Pascal

I think there is a definite lack of craft in the people of my generation that are coming up. Because entertainment and the media are the dominating forces. More than money, more than sex, more than anything. It's entertainment. It's getting your face out there. It's becoming "a star."

I know, for myself, I need to study. But that doesn't mean I'm going to study, because I'm a very undisciplined person when it comes to certain things. I feel that I have a certain amount in me that I'm able to do and I know that there are vast amounts that I need to work on.

But on the other side of the coin, I know a lot of people who spend years and years studying. They have gone to acting school—they have dropped out of high school. But they get on a stage and they choke—they can't say a word. All they can do is work in the classroom, and working in a classroom and working on a stage are completely different things.

John Shea

If you look back at the 20th century, the history of American—acting technique—well, there really wasn't any up until the 1950s. So let's say, from 1900, coming out of the 19th-century American—acting tradition, which was essentially Shakespearean, from John Wilkes Booth and Edwin Booth and Edwin Forrest and so forth, there were basically men who studied in the Shakespearean tradition.

We essentially had the English tradition in America through The Group Theatre, probably to the '40s and '50s. With The Group Theatre and with Clifford Odets, there started a new exploration, even in the late '30s, of Naturalism. There was the concept that you didn't have to be a king to have your story told. You could be a guy who works in a kitchen. You could chew gum, you could smoke cigarettes, you could have holes in the soles of your shoes.

Then, you had to teach actors how to act that way. Everybody thought speaking with a British accent, being royal, was the right way to do it. But suddenly, there are guys from the Bronx who are onstage, writers who are writing characters in the Bronx, and it was OK. As a matter of fact, it was better than an actor who spoke with perfect diction. American techniques were incorporated into [Konstantin] Stanislavsky techniques, and into Strasberg's work and [Sanford] Meisner's.

Now, I think what's happening at the end of the 20th century and the beginning of the 21st is that what we have is a synthesis of the two things. We have the English technique, which I think I remember learning as "working from the outside in." And then, for the American technique, it is "working from inside out." What are your emotions? How do you relate to the play? What kind of memories and things can you bring to this character that brings it alive?

I know that when I'm onstage right now, in this character, if you were to ask me how I brought it to life, it is "the play's the thing." Definitely. I read the character, I read the play over and over. Every night before I go onstage, I'm looking at the lines, I'm discovering something new. I discover that by doing it organically, by reading it and then rehearsing it, and then slowly doing it in the course of rehearsals and performance, things start to happen to you from the inside out.

Daphne Rubin-Vega

I realized after a while, after auditioning and auditioning, that being a natural, as it were, wasn't going to do much with so many amazing talents out there. So, I studied with Bill Esper. He probably doesn't want me to say that publicly. He actually taught me something. I learned that there was a technique—that when you couldn't pull it out of yourself organically, there was technique behind it to do that.

Swoosie Kurtz

I believe in research to a certain extent, as much as it is practical, as much as it will immediately help you apply to the play. I don't think you have to have gouged out your lover's eyes to play Medea. That's our technique. That's where the imagination comes in and that's where our art comes in. If you're playing a doctor or whatever, definitely do as much research as you can.

Tammy Grimes

There is a critical part of you that is always working onstage. There is a part of you that is consciously looking at what you are doing. Some part of your brain is looking at you under a magnifying glass.

Robert Prosky

I heard once, or I read somewhere, that Ralph Richardson occasionally would have a live mouse in his pocket. And the reason why, he said, "To keep my mind off myself!"

Frank Langella

It's instinct, I think first, and then experience. Years and years of getting up and discovering how and in what way you

can hold the audience. How quiet you can get in what theatre you're performing. How loud you can afford to be.
Often, you can be too loud in a performance, not too low.

Mercedes Ruehl

Technique seems to me to have a couple of different mean-
ings. When you've a young actor, one of the things that you
do or feel is a fear of the audience. "They're going to eat
me up!" As a matter of fact, even when you're a middle-
aged actor, some of the time. I remember when I was young,
hiding from the audience. There are two ways you can hide
from the audience. You can hide your face, and you can
hide by speaking softly. So, one part of technique is just
learning not to hide from the audience.

Carole Shelley

A lot of English actors are trained to have too much discipline. When I came to America, I was astounded by the
amount of freedom that the actors had. I came with the technical abilities, but was given the leeway to experiment to feel
free.

Cherry Jones

In Chicago in particular for *A Moon for the Misbegotten*, it
took every ounce of courage I had to get onstage every night.

I was completely constricted and paralyzed. Terrified. I would literally go onstage and pose and say this line and walk over here and pose again and say that line. I knew I had come to New York and would open in this Broadway show. They weren't going to fire me. I was one of the stars. That's the terrible thing about success. They don't fire you because you are part of the money. But there was no way out. I have pride in what I do. So, I had to call upon all that craft I had built up over the years just to get out there.

Jessica Lange

I always had this kind of visual image—whatever is happening backstage, you're getting ready, you're doing this or doing that. And the moment you step onstage it's like being enveloped by a freight train that just comes up behind you. It just picks you up, and until the play is over you are on this track. You are on this ride. All you have to do is open your heart and give yourself up to it. If you want to look at it from a technical point of view, or as poetry, or the universality of the human emotion, or whatever it is, it all just encompasses you and takes you there.

As long as you don't resist it, it delivers you where you have to go.

Martha Plimpton

I want to see the art in the way they [the actors] are being honest, in the choices they make, in the way they move their bodies. How someone is telling a story, with the way that person uses his or her voice, or the arms are used, or the way they address the audience. These are artificial things that we give to a character, to a performance, for effect. And we should have them because that's what draws people in.

I must say, that's what I look for when I go to the theatre. I go for a sense that my mind is being respected, number one. My intelligence is respected and that I am being drawn into a world. That I am having the experience, not just watching someone feel something. That's not terribly interesting to me. I want to feel it.

Frances Sternhagen

Sanford Meisner would always spot where you had not listened or responded, at what moment, and so on. But what I found later was, in terms of character work, for some reason or other, I think people who have a sense of how to be other people, who are not like themselves. I think you either have that or you don't. And I don't think even he could teach people how to do, as John Cleese calls it, "the funny walks."

Michael Crawford

[For *Barnum*] I spent four months with the Big Apple Circus School, which is the equivalent of the Peking Torture Chamber. They have wires and ropes that you hang from and things that you swing from, and one-wheeled bicycles that you put between your legs at ten o'clock in the morning and your life is ruined for three months thereafter. I was told after two lessons this can bring on impotency, but I still pursued it.

It was quite a hard task. I felt, as with everything I seem to get involved with, I like to become very involved so that it is as authentic as it can possibly be, and to make the audience believe that if I weren't a fully trained circus performer of twenty-five years, at least I was someone who understood the enthusiasm of a circus performer—which is unlike anything any of us can know.

A dancer's life is the hardest I have ever witnessed in our profession. But a circus life is harder than that.

Tony Randall

All of us believe that you work simply and try to find the role, and leave yourself alone and let it happen to you.

Paul Muni did exactly the opposite. He began Acting Big, from the very first rehearsal. And it was just terrible all this acting he did. And with readings of the lines and overdoing everything. It was just horrible. There were fifty-five actors in the company. And we looked at each other, *This is Paul Muni?*

Well, we knew he was a great actor. But it was a scaffold he built. He felt comfortable. Also, he did other strange things. He put on complete make-up for every rehearsal. He bought six hundred dollars of make-up. You cannot use up six hundred dollars worth of make-up in a career.

One day, he was in the second act of *Inherit the Wind,* and he couldn't learn his lines, which is very unusual for an actor who's been in the business since childhood. My experience has been that actors who have trouble learning their lines started late. But those who began early could learn fast. Now, he had been an actor since his parents had been actors. And he could not learn his lines. It was just embarrassing. One day, in the middle of this oration, the script flew in the air! Sweat burst from him! And his eyes and voice went, and he was a wild animal up and down the stage, pacing like a tiger, screaming! The speech lasted about ten minutes. We were left speechless. And there was one old guy named Louis Hector, he leaned over to me and said, "That baby can act!"

Jeffrey Wright

There's something very exciting, just the actor being loud. It's very freeing in some way for the voice and for the breath, and for everything. I really find it exciting when I can almost see the sound reverberate off the back of the house.

Blythe Danner

I do lots of reading. Working on *The Deep Blue Sea*, I read the Terence Rattigan biography. There's lots of emotional stuff and this very rich material. I try to leave myself as open as possible but also to do as much preparation as possible. Mostly, reading. I must admit, I snuck a look at the BBC production that they did in London, which was very helpful. When I was a young actor, I never would deign to do such a thing. I was a purist. I had to come up with all of it, from my own complete preparation. But as I've gotten older I've thought, "Why not steal from the best?"

Elizabeth Franz

[The core moment comes] from reading. Reading, reading the play, with your fellow actors. And as we're sitting around—how long would we work around this table? And we read and discussed it, and said, "Now, this moment is this and this moment is that." And then, when we get up on our feet, and then the characters become developed inside of us, before we know it, those moments are there. They're magical, in a way, through the eyes of the other actors.

Vanessa Redgrave

We all work with our physical accoutrements and try to think, *Well, what does such a person say, how does she walk? How does she breathe? What clothes does he or she like? How does what's inside them express itself?* Well, it can only express itself in its connection with objects outside. But I sometimes find exactly that problem, that I've made a scaffolding that I'm imprisoned inside. I'll get the wig, I'll get it all worked out to convince myself that this is how this person would be. But perhaps sometimes I make some bad mistakes when I do that, which wouldn't be surprising. It's become a scaffolding that I've got to throw away, since I can't breathe through it.

Joel Grey

There was no such character [as the emcee in *Cabaret*] in [Christopher] Isherwood. One day, we had been rehearsing for about three weeks, and everybody was happy and it was fine. But I wasn't. I didn't know who he [the character] was. And so I decided that day to do it like someone I had seen in a nightclub once, someone for whom I had such distaste. I thought, *That is the cheapest, cruddiest performer I have ever seen,* and it really stuck with me. It was a song-and-dance comedian, oddly enough. And I thought to myself, *I can't bear what he does!*

So, I decided that day to do that, to do everything that he did that I so hated and was repulsed by.

I finished doing the number, I remember very clearly, and I ran offstage afterward into the corner and I started to cry. I was humiliated. I had done it in front of everybody and it was so painful to acknowledge that I knew about this. And also, maybe in some way, I was killing somebody. There was something dark about what I was using. And Hal Prince came over and said, "That's it!" And I had to live with it. And then, come to love it.

Lynn Redgrave

When I did *The Three Sisters* [by Anton Chekhov], it so happened that right before doing it I had the opportunity to see three totally separate productions in different parts of the world. And you bet I went to them. And I came up with a

Masha that was not like any that I saw. But I learned something from everybody.

John Lithgow

Playing a woman? I had played a girl, tied to the railroad tracks in Boy Scout camp when I was eleven. But beyond that, I'd never played a woman. I was dying to play the part [of Roberta Muldoon in the film *The World According to Garp*]. I had read the novel of *Garp* and remembered the character very, very vividly. I auditioned for it and was hired eight months later.

I was very interested in this transsexual woman, Jan Morris, years before. I found her a very captivating woman. She wrote an autobiography and did book tours and interviews. I remember just being fascinated by all that she had to say. I'd read the book, never dreaming that I would play a transsexual years on down the line.

I didn't ever feel that this should be a highly acted role. I thought it should be a very low-profile, kind of calm and ordinary person, and just let the extraordinary fact of my size and presence—the difference between myself and the other characters—take care of the kind of comedy, the eccentricity, the bizarre.

I became very maternal, a very kind person, kind of compassionate. But not artificial—in fact, more genuine than any other part I've ever played. As such, preparation for it, assuming a whole bunch of mannerisms, that was less an issue than it usually is, which is a paradox because, God knows, it's the most unusual part I've ever played.

Brian Stokes Mitchell

[With *Ragtime*], I had a book from which to work. And if you ever have that opportunity, it is the best place to go since there is, of course, so much more information in a book than you'll ever see onstage. You get into the heads of people. Also, I was reading whatever I could on the time period: it wasn't a time that I was incredibly familiar with.

So, I read books on Booker T. Washington, on W. E. B. Du Bois, who was kind of Malcolm X at the time to Booker T. Washington's Martin Luther King Jr. Any books on the period, I think, when you're doing a period piece, you have to perform sort of *subtractive consciousness*. There's so much that we know now, through just having television and the media, which people didn't know back then. It was a less-familiar time. People were less familiar with each other. So, part of it was trying to understand the consciousness and the head of the people.

Chris Bauer

When it comes down to constructing a character through a series of actions, it's just all about, *What are they doing?* And *Who are they?* comes after that.

Willem Dafoe

I'm a person who prefers doing things as opposed to saying things. So, I would probably always respond much more to actions than I would to the text.

Dana Ivey

I'm a Southerner, and it's [*The Last Night of Ballyhoo*] a Southern play. I think we all know that people think of Southern expression as being something very musical and lilting. I hear things when I read something. I sort of hear the way it should be, and then I can do the inflection and the rhythm, and the timing that I feel is correct for what the character and the situation are, and it leads me back into the meaning of a play like this.

Some of my readings have changed because going from that initial understanding, which was correct, I have found a way to make it even more correct, deepening it. But the music was there first, and it shapes the whole structure of the play.

Jessica Lange

I think it's the most dangerous thing if you start thinking in terms of arias. Then, you really are sunk. I think what we're talking about, "poetry," is probably a misnomer. I think what we're talking about is the musicality of his [Tennessee Williams's] language. You can't paraphrase, you can't flip words. You can't ignore punctuation.

Now, Sam Shepard has a sense of music, but it's rock 'n' roll music. Williams has a sense of music and it's very specific to him. You have to honor that. I don't think you have to be conscious of this so-called poetry. But you have to honor the music of his language.

Andre de Shields

It seems to me that it is the music that we are trying to hear in whatever effort we make in the theatre, whether we're reading the play for the first time or speaking the words for the first time, or it's the first rehearsal. Or, as I did recently, worked outside of my visible genre, as a song-and-dance man. I had an opportunity to work at the Oasis Theatre in the role of Willy Loman in *Death of a Salesman.* Quite a stretch for me. But the first thing I looked for was the music in Arthur Miller, the music in the life of Willy Loman, the music that matched this man's journey.

Brian Stokes Mitchell

I've been really fortunate in that I generally forget and lines of music will drop out. The other day, I was singing, "Make Them Hear You," and the word didn't come out at all. I had no idea where it was and when it was coming up. I was thinking, *I have no idea what this word is,* and I'm singing the song, *OK, what's this word? . . . OK, I'll just not sing it.* And I dropped the word and just went on with the song. And you hope nobody knows.

For about a week I had these huge anxiety attacks. I begin the second act [of *Ragtime*] with a soliloquy number. I remember, for about four performances, I'm standing on the steps going, *What? I have no idea what I'm supposed to sing. I have no idea what the words are.* And nobody's around me to ask and I can't ask anybody. You just go into panic mode. And, of course, that's the worst thing you can do.

So, you try to breathe. And you trust that the character is in your body. I'd already done four-, five-hundred live performances of the show. And you just trust that it's in your body and you can get out there. I just do the tabula-rasa thing with my head. *OK, blank slate. I don't even know who I am.* Then, something happens and it just comes out.

Brian Dennehy

[In Willy Loman], I was fascinated by the element of mental illness. That was the study I did. I did a lot of work on depression and bipolar presentation, what happens when somebody is losing control and stuff like that, and is swinging back and forth.

Marian Seldes

The greatest tool of all is to observe life around you, and your life inside you. That's easy to say. But there are times in an actor's life where there's nothing there. But whenever you travel, whenever you watch children, whenever you watch animals—I'm no good at percentages—but a great, great deal of what I know and feel about the theatre is from watching other people, from being an observer and a thief.

Frank Langella

A myth that I think should be broken down about being an actor is that you should live a monk-like existence, or an existence that is free of stress. The more stressful your life is, the more complicated it is, the more people there are in it, the more you have children and marriages and love affairs and arguments and fights, the more difficult the day is, the moment you get to the theater and you have that . . . with me, it's just about thirty seconds. As I get older, I know I need less and less preparation. When I was younger, I would think, *Well, I have to clear my day.* It's nonsense. By the time I went on, it was all gone.

The more complicated your life, the better an actor you are, I think.

Alan Alda

I understudied people a couple of times, and I found it was very interesting to watch somebody up on the stage playing my part. I wouldn't have played it anything at all the way they played it. I would not go for certain things that they did, which I saw didn't work.

Patrick Stewart

I thought for a long time about putting together a slim volume of instruction for actors because there were things that nobody said to me. I had to find them out by trial and error, by watching other actors. I've thought of approaching actors to give me some of their tips. For instance, one of them I firmly believe in is never touching the furniture when you're onstage. Ever! Unless you actually have an action that has something to do with furniture. But never touch it because touching the furniture is weak. Never point onstage, either. Pointing is also very weak.

F. Murray Abraham

All this stuff is just theory. It's true, you can talk all you want to about it. But there's only one place finally to learn. That's up on the stage with your hair on fire.

Carole Shelley

Study and become a doctor or a lawyer and you have a diploma that gives you sort of a guarantee for life. Get a diploma from an acting school and you have nothing. It's a risk.

3

Auditioning

Frank Langella

We're always auditioning. You're actually auditioning when you're in a play, every night.

F. Murray Abraham

I'd like to mention one thing about the audition process. It's the same thing, essentially, as the acting process. It's bigger and it's bolder, but essentially it counts on you using whatever it is you have to offer.

There's only one thing that will ever sell you, and that's the thing that makes you so completely individual, apart from everyone else. That's the thing that these people want to see. They want you to tell them the answer, because they don't know the answer. And if you go in and try to find that thing in yourself, yourself alone, which you have to offer, you'll come out of the audition; and if you don't get it, it doesn't matter. You have really done the right thing.

Irene Worth

I auditioned for a film yesterday. That's all I have to say. I rush to say, I didn't think I got it—but anyway, I did. It's indescribably difficult to audition.

Frances Sternhagen

I remember auditioning for Sidney Lumet and Paddy Chayefsky for *Network,* for Beatrice Straight's part. And both of them burst into tears at my audition. I was told by my agent, "Well, they loved what you did, but you're not round enough." Well, Faye Dunaway, if you remember, she's kind of angular, and they needed somebody who was rounder. But I'm glad I auditioned.

Nell Carter

How did I get in? I would buy the paper for casting and if it called for a redhead, I would buy a red wig and go! And as long as I had the wig, and if the stage manager would tell other people, "No," I would say, "This is my hair. I bought it. I'm staying!" And that's how I got a lot of jobs.

I had a chance when they did *The Corn Is Green*. I wanted to meet Joshua Logan and Bette Davis—there was nothing that was going to keep me out of there. And Mrs. Watty was supposed to be a Welsh woman with red hair. Well, she turned out to be very black, very fat, and with some real kinks because I got that role. I went out there, red wig on, and I did the audition. And the casting director said, "She can have it!"

Michael Nouri

I've been in the business long enough to be somewhat acquainted with how people think, and it really comes down to common sense. If I were a producer or a director, and if I were sitting out there looking at a young person that I was not sure about, if this person didn't have a body of work as a singer, and this person were in an audition room with a piano, I'd ask, *How is he going to be with one of the biggest stars on the Broadway stage? Will he freeze? Can he carry it? Is he present? What's he like with an orchestra?*

George Rose

There's an awful lot of time wasted at auditions. The older I get, the more I realize that there is only one talent worth having for any director, and that is the talent to get the right actors in the first place. Know what you want. This plowing through, seeing millions of people, really means that you don't know your job.

Jay Binder

It seems easy, what I want to say, but it's very true. When an actor auditions for a play or a musical, we don't make the decision. They walk in the room, open their mouths—they're that part and they own it. That's what you look for. Because when someone walks in the room or walks on the stage and reads a part, there can be no argument amongst the creative staff, because [that person] owns it.

Estelle Parsons

My husband used to say I was crazy, because I was the only person he ever met who liked to audition. But for me, it's a performance.

Daniel Davis

I think it's the worst experience in life. Sort of a public execution. I always try to go in with a very strong idea of the character and the material. I usually try to have in my mind a fairly strong objective to play. I say all of this so that I have something to do when I get in the room. At the same time, I try to keep myself completely open and available to a director who may like where I'm coming from but wants me to go another way. I think it's an unnatural thing to have to do, to go in and persuade somebody that, after thirty-five or forty years of acting, that you know what you're doing.

Elizabeth Franz

You have to have a great passion for it. A true passion, and a great belief in yourself because you're not going to get that belief from other people. And you just never take "No" for an answer. And if you really have that passion, you will be fulfilled eventually, but it's hard.

Gregory Hines

I've always felt insecure going into auditions. I have tremendous respect for the casting process. However, I know most of the time casting people are not really sure what they're looking for—but when they see it, they can recognize it. It's just that for me, I think in my heart of hearts, I always resented the fact that I couldn't just walk in and they would say, "You're the man we want." There would be fifteen or twenty other men there and I would be aware of their talent, and that would just make me feel insecure. Even if it were not a three-hundred-person cattle call, the fact that there are some people trying to get the part makes it difficult to relax and do one's best work.

But after auditioning for a few things, and maybe staying in the running for a couple of callbacks and getting a few, I began to get a bit more secure at auditioning.

Michael Crawford

I don't like auditions at all. Some people are really good at auditions, and once they've got the part they're actually terrible because they're professionals at auditions. They're very good sight readers. As soon as they put that script down, they freeze.

I auditioned years ago for a musical in England. It was in Liverpool, for a well-known gentleman—and they can be quite cruel at auditions. There are always those, "Hello, are you out there?" You're standing there and they ask, "All right, Michael, are you going to sing something for us?" I said, "Yes, I, uh, 'On the Street Where You Live,'" and he said, "Oh, great." And without even seeing you could hear, "Oh God, it's the twentieth guy that's tried to sing 'On the Street Where You Live.'"

There's always this dreadful point where you get to the middle section, which goes high, and then they ask, "Which key would you like?" The key to me was either the front door or the back door. I didn't know what a key was. I couldn't actually read music.

By the time I got to "I have often," you know it's wrong. The hand is gone and the head is shaking and the legs have gone.

When I got to the middle, I went way off, saying, "That's very, very high there and we actually started in the wrong key." He said, "We guessed that, Michael. Do you know anything else?" And I could hear laughter, and then—I mean, this is a funny, tragic story, because this happens to so many artists and it still reminds me now—my bottom lip begins to go because I was crying. I had made a complete fool of myself and this was my life. This was my life they were playing with out there.

Daphne Rubin-Vega

[I learned of the audition for *Rent*] from my agent. She knows that I'm a singer, and she said, "There is a rock opera based on *La Bohème.*" Immediately, I wanted to have nothing to do with it. I felt that I wanted to keep my music and my acting separate. This was just my choice. I didn't really question it. And she said, "Well, it's a rock opera. The music is brand-spanking new. And Mimi is a junkie S&M dancer with AIDS." And I said, "That sounds great." I didn't go in there ravenous. I just went in giving it what I could.

John Schneider

I would have crawled over hot coals to audition for *Grand Hotel.* And did! And I had to come from the mountains, I live in the mountains so I had to go quite a distance. [There are] maybe two or three things that come up in your acting life that you just have to do.

The question after an audition, from your agent, from whomever, is always, "Well, how did you do?" In any other business, you'd say, "I did great," and the job would follow. In this business, you can do a terrific audition, and not get the job.

Kate Burton

I did audition for *Some Americans Abroad*. My experience, though, was that I hadn't read the play when I auditioned. I had it for two hours. I didn't know the characters. I was the last person they saw and they offered me the part a few hours later. So then I read the play, and that was a really scary experience. I didn't like it when I first read it. And I thought, *Oh, God.* And then I read it again. And then I decided, *Yeah, I think I'll give this a shot.*

Matthew Broderick

My father once told me, when I auditioned for something and I didn't get the part, I thought, *I screwed up,* and he said, "Maybe they did." So, I think that's something to keep in mind when you're starting. Somebody doesn't cast you, there's no reason to think they're right all the time. Keep that in mind.

Judith Ivey

I was offered the role of Patrice in *A Fair Country* and didn't audition. I spent the first week waiting for them to fire me. And I realized the luxury of auditioning is that it's an affirmation that what brought you in the room is what they want.

Gregory Hines

In addition to those feelings of self-confidence and how we have to prepare ourselves to audition, we also have to have tremendous aggression. I think it takes tremendous aggression to try to get to work in this business. A lot of other talented people, not that many opportunities, and it takes something more than just when somebody says, "Thank you."

Patti Cohenour

It's an agonizing thing for me. I had four auditions for *The Phantom of the Opera*. The most specific one was my first time out to sing for everyone and Hal Prince had not seen me in at least three years. We hadn't really gotten to talk, and I was shaking so badly. He came running up onstage and gave me a big hug, and he says, "I thought that was the subway going underneath the theatre—it's you!"

So, no, I don't function well in the audition process. But I learn from them. I definitely learn from the process. But I have yet to perfect the way to handle it. I still get nervous.

Audra McDonald

I kept missing musical theatre a lot. I snuck away and I left school for six months and did *The Secret Garden* tour. Then, I got the call to come in and audition for *Carousel*. And I auditioned six times. After fainting at my final callback—I also fainted when I auditioned for *Show Boat,* I'm good at that. Oh, I fainted—I sang, "Darling Mr. Snow." Boom! I fainted. I sang "Bill" for the *Show Boat* audition. And I sang, "He's just my. . . ." Bang! I fainted for that.

Lucie Arnaz

God forbid you ever audition on a Thanksgiving holiday because everybody leaves town right after the audition. I went back to my hotel and called. And they said, "Well, they've all gone away for the Thanksgiving holidays, so we won't know until Monday." I had to stay for four extra [days], in case they wanted me to come back.

And Monday morning, they called and they said, "No, you didn't get the part." And I said, "No. Yes, I did." I [then] said, "Wait a minute, find out why." They were ready to tell me *no* and go on. And I found out by asking and asking and asking that it was Cy Coleman who had said, "I don't think she can belt." I said, "Well, no one asked me to belt. They specifically said 'ballad.' " I asked where he was and they said he was going back to L.A. I then went back to L.A., found out where he was, forced him to sit down and listen to me sing again, and I got the part. I sang every song Ethel Merman ever recorded.

Jerry Orbach

Lotte Lenya told me that most people in a singing audition will sing to the exit signs somewhere in the mezzanine. What happens is, if you start singing right at [people], they become the ones who are a little nervous.

Lonette McKee

Sometimes, you do find out [why you did not get the role]. I like to know why I didn't get it. I think it's important. Was it because I came in with a funny attitude that day because I argued with the cabdriver? Is it because I'm too tall? Is it because I'm black? Is it because I'm not black enough? Did I not read well? Did I not sing well? Or, none of the above?

Maximilian Schell

I always remember Montgomery Clift, who is for me not only a friend but also maybe the greatest film actor America ever made. When he read for *Judgment at Nuremberg,* he read [in a complete monotone] on the first reading. You could see that while he was reading, he was destroying every part he had played before. He started from chaos, from nowhere. And I think that's the right way to do it.

I taught at USC and most of the students want to know, "How shall I do an audition?" I cannot teach that. I said, "Don't do it if you can."

Charlotte d'Amboise

I don't think you ever, *ever,* conquer auditioning, or ever control it the way you want. It's a struggle constantly, and will always be—you learn as you go.

Ann Duquesnay

I hate to audition. My hands get so clammy when I walk into an audition. I just hate it. And sometimes, they can be so disillusioning because you get in there and you sing, and there are nine people sitting at the table. When you finish, they're all applauding. And you wait for the call, and you don't get it.

Heather Headley

I remember somebody had told me that every "No" leads to a "Yes." And so, if I was not told "No" to on certain auditions, I would not have been available to get *Aida*.

I think that is empowering in itself, and that no matter what happens today, when I leave this room, I'm still Heather and I'm still good at what I do. I still need to learn a lot, but I did the best I could this day, and this was not my journey. My journey's coming up. That's how I get through the rejection of it.

Faith Prince

I don't think I had ever really known how difficult auditioning was until I sat on the other side of the table, when I was looking at other people auditioning. That was the most painful thing I have ever been through. And I thought, *What*

made me think I could even get in this business and get a job?
I have this sort of thing where I just stay in my lane. I think,
Oh, I'm going to get to the finish line. It was a really good
coping skill for me, early on, because I thought, *I am the
girl you need for this part. I am the one!* And I would go in
with that sort of strong center.

Rob Marshall

Dancers audition in a group, perhaps forty people there; he
[Bob Fosse] would go around whispering, "Thank you very
much," specifically to the ones that weren't right for the part.
And it's embarrassing in front of people that you know.

Marian Seldes

Once, in California, a man with orange-leather shoes put
them up on the desk. And I said, "I really can't do this until
you put your feet down." I was very young then. I dared.

But I didn't see—I mean, we're actors. Part of what we
do is audition. And part of what we do is get reviewed. It's
all part of our life, and we have to accept all of it.

A couple of things I've auditioned for, I've felt as if I've
played them anyway. Do you know what I mean? I prepared
so well, and I've enjoyed it. But I didn't get [the part].

I have never gone to a play or seen a play that I auditioned for that I thought they should have chosen me. I've
always understood later why. And it's not necessarily you.

It's the other actor you play the scene with or something. You can teach yourself not to be so upset.

Kathleen Marshall

The hard thing is that there are people that you love and you respect and [of whom] you're a fan. But your responsibility is to the show and to the production that you are doing. And people who are not just actors but also friends, you think, *These are people I adore but I can't cast them.* You have to do what is right for the play. It's often very clear. And I think a lot of actors are going to think, *But I'm an actor! I'm flexible. What do you need? I can give you what you need.* [My answer is,] "Sure. But you know what? This other person is closer to it—to who they really are, in their real sensibility." It's very hard not to disappoint people, and you know you're always disappointing people.

John Shea

Auditions are very mysterious, mystical times and you deal with what happens. I think that there is a very delicate line between under-preparedness and over-preparedness. If you memorize something, you are suggesting a performance in the audition that you are not capable of giving, and so I tend to read things. I used to go in with the whole play memorized just to give one little speech. But then I found out I was raising expectations in the producer's and director's minds of what I was actually capable of doing. I also found out that I had already preconceived my performance. Instead, now—even if I'm tremendously familiar with it and know basically what is going on—I read it. I half-memorize and want things to happen spontaneously onstage rather than having preconceived something. So, the director then thinks that there is a place to work with this person, and I haven't frozen myself into a performance. It took me a long time to learn that.

I insist upon auditioning. It is only in working with the director in an audition that you know that you and the director can really work together, that you speak, somehow, the same language. He'll say, "Fine, you have the role." And I'll say, "No, let's read some scenes." You're really testing each other. You're also auditioning the director, as he's auditioning you. You are really auditioning the possibility of working together, and having the best kind of chemistry, the kind of language that will allow the play to come to life.

At times, I'll get into a situation where the director will say, "Well, I don't know. I don't care." I don't want to work with that sort of person. I want to work with somebody that will really probe.

An audition time is a magical time. It's like the first date. You're not married to the situation yet.

Maximilian Schell

One of my colleagues said to me once, "When I go into an audition, I look around and I say, 'Ten or twenty years from now, you will all be dead, and I will still be alive!'" And that gave him the courage to do it.

Nell Carter

Pick up the paper and every role you see in that, go up for it. Go up for every role. They will eventually think you are crazy and let you in, or you will get a chance but eventually you will get around. They either think you're so dumb and let you in for free, or they'll give you a chance. I'm serious. Go for it! No one can stop you.

4

Playwright and Director

Kathleen Chalfant

Our job is to communicate what the writer meant to say.

Hal Linden

One doesn't have free rein on the stage when one creates a role. You still have a writer and a director saying, "No, do it this way. How about this? And try this."

Andrea Martin

I'm going to rewrite Terrence McNally? I'm going to rewrite *Lips Together*, [*Teeth Apart*]? "Terrence, I got a new line for you!"

It's all about fear. It's all about, *I don't know if I can really do what he wrote.*

Frank Langella

The sooner you learn that you're a vessel, the quicker your fear goes away. Because when you're younger, you sort of go out there thinking, *Look at me! Watch me!* But once you understand you're a vessel for the playwright your fear disappears.

Robert Prosky

There is a tradition, however, that actors generally don't speak directly to the playwright. Generally you talk to the director, and the director will talk to the playwright.

Marian Seldes

I think that if you can find a way to do the play the way the playwright wrote it, and feel the part you play, you can show this in rehearsal. You don't have to talk about it, really. I think the task is really to fulfill what the playwright wrote.

Edward Albee

We had a problem during the original Broadway production [of *Tiny Alice*], with John Gielgud playing Brother Julian.

And he began rehearsals by saying, "I don't understand a word of this play. Not a word!"

Robert Prosky

The playwright is the artist. But I think the actor is the artist as well. I think actors can expand on a play and make it work better.

Incidentally, as far as changing lines, I find that it's the lines that I don't understand and I don't really know why they're in there that are the clue, that are the key to the play and to the performance, the understanding of the character.

Linda Lavin

To work on a new play with a living playwright is rare for us. In television, you work with living writers. But they change often. To work with Neil Simon—who is such a craftsperson, so skillful, and [have him] watch you and never blame you when it doesn't work [is an inspiration]. He always takes the blame. The collaboration is thrilling.

Alan Alda

You don't rewrite anything when you're in a Neil Simon play.

Richard Easton

I say to young actors, when they ask, "What do you do if the director wants you to do something and you don't want to do it?" Well, you do what you want to. What can the director say? You're out there and doing it, and you say, "Oh, sorry, I forgot again."

Ian McKellen

Constantly be objective about yourself is the best advice I have for anybody. My plan in university was only to work with good directors. The actors I admire are those who dare to do something that perhaps they aren't quite willing to do. If you are working with Shakespeare, you have to dare practically every syllable of the way, it is so demanding.

Mark Hamill

The best directors have a clear idea of what they need from the performers. They cast it and pretty much step back. The director becomes a father figure, a confessor, almost a psychiatrist. He's probably the most crucial person there.

Joel Grey

I did a production of Ibsen's *When We Dead Awaken,* which Robert Wilson directed. It was an opportunity to work in a completely different way from anything I had ever done. It was all about music and structure, and dance and movement, and the acting was the last thing you ever came to. And it was difficult. But ultimately, it was very exciting to be in a new form. And I knew that it spoke in the way that Robert Wilson, who is a great theatre artist, meant for it to speak, and we were all part of that expression. But it was terrifying since it had nothing to do with anything that any of us had trained for.

Heather Headley

[*Aida* went through] everybody. The set designers, the directors, choreographer, everybody. And it was tough. These people hired me and I'm watching them go. There was a lot of hurt and breaking with me.

I had to keep the core of Aida but not insult the new director by saying, "Well, this is what I did before." I had to remember her core—but not to bring that to the table; and to be open to whatever he was going to bring to my table as well.

Lynn Redgrave

I like directors who create an atmosphere—to be hopeless, foolish, wonderful—to try anything.

Colm Wilkinson

I've always believed that the action of genius is simplicity. Trevor Nunn and John Caird have this facility to bring the best out of people without interference. They just let you do your thing, but mold what you are doing into what is wanted. People who speak in simple terms know where it's at. Trevor Nunn has this innocence, this conception of theatre, this approach. He talks so innocently, like a child, of what he wants you to do. He's for real.

Martha Plimpton

I think the director is almost the most important thing in bringing people together. We all come from these sort of disparate backgrounds with these varying ideas of what the play should be, and what we want to do with the play when we come into the room. And maybe we know we have to keep our minds open, but we have a plan since we took this role—there is something in there that we need to look at or explore.

Everyone comes into the room with his or her own version of that. And a truly great ensemble, I think, is formed when the director can bring all of these people together on the first day, or maybe the second. It should be in the first week. It should be early. Everyone lays out his or her vision of the world, of the story that we want to tell, the story we are here to tell. They open an umbrella and welcome everyone in the cast into it, and shelter them in that. That's not to say that it oughtn't to be a fluid and elastic vision. Of course, it always should be. But it's so important to establish that early, so that we all know we're in the service of the same thing, so that we all know our mandate in a strange way.

Mercedes Ruehl

You do have to become director-proof. What you need is a great third eye.

Ann Duquesnay

Listening and looking, you can learn so much from people who think they are not giving anything. Just by looking, and working with fabulous musical directors, working with fabulous directors directing me, I have gotten to where I am.

Diahann Carroll

I was so young when I worked with Peter Brook that, frankly, I didn't know what the hell he was talking about most of the time.

Frank Langella

It's frightening how few directors love us.

Adam Pascal

The music aspect of *Rent* always came easily to me, obviously, because this is what I do. The acting aspect of it didn't come so easily, although it was much easier than it could have been, given the circumstances. I was very lucky to have Michael Greif and Tim Weil and Jonathan Larson to nurture me, and really to help me find this character and find myself as an actor.

It's very easy for a director to take a first-time actor like me and say, "All right, do this. Stand here. Do this. Act this way. Be happy. Be sad." But Michael didn't do that. He was very nurturing and very open, and basically allowed me to find myself as an actor, and I think that's why it works. He didn't force me to any particular direction. He let me find that direction myself.

Jim Dale

A play is made up of, you name it, ten-thousand, twenty-thousand moments. That's all theatre is, moments that are created during a rehearsal period. The director has his own idea as to where he wants the play to go. But within that idea, he allows you certain freedoms. And I suppose that every night after two or three or four weeks, or two or three or four months, one doesn't go out there to do something different. One goes out there to polish that particular moment that you didn't hit on last night.

But you go to see any production, or the director will, and see it at eye level. Then, over the months, it would be at that [lower] level. But you won't agree. Because, you see, gradually you've changed your performance slightly. The director knows since he's been away for so long. He comes back and you realize, *Yes, it has been dropping. I needed that.*

I needed that push. I needed the director to come in because it's his baby. We took over but it's his baby and he knows where it should be. That's what he wanted.

Martha Plimpton

No actor, I think, wants to belittle or insult a playwright by assuming that she could tell him what the play is about. And no director or actor should expect a playwright to be his own dramaturge. That's incredibly unfair. A playwright is there to put words on the page. It's the director's job to find the ways to articulate that theatrically.

Richard Dreyfuss

There is an old saw in the theatre, or at least I believe there is, which is that the writer knows best first, the director knows best second, but ultimately the actor knows best.

Mercedes Ruehl

In theatre, no director, no editor can come on and say, "Take it again. Don't do that. Let's do it from this angle, you know, there." You're out there telling the story the way Homer told the story around the fire. Beginning, middle, ending. Nobody interrupts. It's a great feeling of power.

5

Bringing a Role to Life

Carole Shelley

I was sent this tiny, thin script and it made me weep. I wanted to do this play and so I showed it to my agent, who thought it was dreadful. It turned out to be *The Elephant Man.* I felt that the disrobing called for in the script was one of the least-gratuitous moments ever and I wanted to do it. The desire was there but I was not as free as a lot of people are because, I suppose, I'm older.

Rehearsal period was a marvelous, exciting period. There was an aura about it. I couldn't remove my blouse, which is done back to the audience, until the dress rehearsal when I had imagined a very thick, impenetrable fourth wall. I was shaking with nerves. I went home, made a pot of tea, and wondered why I was so nervous. I had a revelation: Why should it be any easier for Carole Shelley than it was for Madge Kendal?

Nell Carter

I believe rehearsal is very important since you start doing things and—you improvise something, and it's funny. And then your fellow actor lets it go, all of a sudden, it's a part of the show, and you want to say, *Back up.* So, I think rehearsal is very important.

Natasha Richardson

When we actually came to start rehearsals, John Kander, who'd had difficult experiences with past Sally Bowles's vocal abilities, got nervous and said he wanted me to come and sing for him for the revival of *Cabaret.*

I went along to his place and I had the flu, and I had not worked on it at all. I didn't know the songs, really. And they said, "OK, well just start singing the songs." And I started to sing, and there was this deathly silence in the room. I thought, *Oh, I don't think this feels good at all. They're not exactly jumping up and down with joy.*

Finally, we got to "Mein Herr," and everybody sat up a little and they said, "Oh, how come you sing that song like that?" And I said, "Because I know this song and I feel comfortable singing it since I know it."

All I know is that, had it been an audition, with the four songs I sang before we got to "Mein Herr," and after one song, they would have said, "Thank you very much. On to the next!"

Marian Seldes

Well, the Lunts, of course, are famous for constantly rehearsing up until the last day, and for being together, of course, all the time, and therefore discussing the performance.

And Alfred Lunt said to his wife, the brilliant Lynn Fontanne, "Why do I miss that laugh on that line? Why do I?" And she said, "When you ask for the sugar?" And he said, "Yes."

And she said to him, "Alfred, darling, you're not getting the laugh because you are asking for the laugh, not for the sugar!"

Edward Herrmann

Generally, I like to walk in with a tabula rasa. I like to start from scratch with the play. Obviously, I read the play quite a few times and get an idea of what I think this is about. But you want the rehearsals to generate and percolate, and get stuff going since you can discover things in rehearsal that you didn't expect. I've found it not so wise to make up your mind exactly how you want to play it before you get in.

Mercedes Ruehl

It's an eternally humbling job, acting. You can invest certain material with the same part of your soul, the same heart, the same emotion, the same [everything], but the actual material itself is not as fortunately composed as the [Anton] Chekhov play you did last year, which you gave the same investment to, and it flew up to heaven.

Richard Thomas

So much of what's terrific about being a human being, in a stage space, is that you bring the space around you to life, not just your own performance here, but you can make real the whole space around you.

6

Working in an Ensemble

Dana Ivey

To be an actor, you have to have some innate gift, whatever it is. Whether you go through formal training or not, you have the intelligence and the sensitivity to grasp, to teach yourself as you go along and learn from other people. Given that you have this ability, then you have to have the experience of working with other people, to have those failures or successes that show your own parameters, how to accomplish what it is that you as the individual artist in this teamwork situation need to accomplish each time and how you serve your team, and how you serve the writer and yourself.

Eddie Albert

I was at the Tony Awards the year that *A Chorus Line* was up, and I was backstage waiting to go on. Watching these kids and the unbelievable life and joy that they had in working together was a joy in itself. Whenever one would win something, the place would go mad.

I had just come back from the West Coast, and I thought, *This is what it's all about. This is what I've missed.* My wife said afterward, "The history of creative art is clear. There is a Renaissance. There is a Left Bank. There's before the war. And so on. You've got to be in the milieu. You've got to be working with each other and swapping ideas, and crying with each other, and fighting with each other. You learn and learn, and you get some kind of inner spiritual drive in the thing."

Rick Lyon

One of the hardest things about this show [*Avenue Q*], regardless of everything else—the choreography and learning the lines and the songs and the music—one of the hardest things is not the choreography exactly, but the staging of the way that those puppets get passed back and forth between two people. Because we have puppeteers who are playing two different characters, and sometimes their characters appear onstage together. How you make that happen, and how you make the puppets shift back and forth, is an extraordinarily complicated traffic pattern.

Vanessa Redgrave

Well, I think it's an awful jungle, for many reasons, especially for the young people. And I think the young and the older people have a lot of courage. It's a horrendous business. And it says a lot for human beings, the fact that for moments, when you're working together, before you get it on, for moments on the stage, for moments in the audience, you do make something close to what it should really be like.

Richard Thomas

Everyone coming together every night to tell the whole story creates a great feeling of ensemble for me, and a feeling of family. No question, for me there's a familial hook in my love, my need for the theatre.

7

Staying Fresh

Marian Seldes

It's always fresh. I don't know anyone in the theatre who isn't dedicated to the performance every day. If I did, I'd pull away. It never occurs to me, if I'm in a long run, to think of how it was the last time, to go backward.

George Rose

Keeping fresh is a problem. One begins to rely more and more on audiences. If audiences come with some kind of expectation in mind and some kind of willingness to participate with the actors, there is really no problem in keeping fresh. Every audience is slightly different. One of the greatest dangers in a long run is to stop listening to one's fellow actors. Keeping a performance fresh is a very conscious thing—every night.

Tony Tanner

Long runs are unnatural. It is natural for man to change. But this is not what the audience wants, it is not what the producers want, it is not what the directors want, it is not what the authors want. They want it to stay the same. They want as nearly as possible for you to re-create the thing over and over and over again. There is a terrible tension there because the audience wants to see the same show that others saw before them, and you want something fresh. I see actors trying different things just to try to break themselves out of what they see as rigid patterns. It is always fresh for the audience even though you have seen it many, many times.

Lucie Arnaz

If a show's been running a long time, six months, any new blood is an infusion. It wakes you up while you're out there. It's a new reading. No matter how good a performance, you can use a little wake up.

John Shea

You go through peaks and valleys. Anybody who's been in a long run will know that there's a period of discovery at the beginning, which is exhilarating. Then, you plateau into a period of repetition and boredom. And then you break through. If you stay long enough and you're still searching, you break through into another period of discovery sometime into the run.

Tom Hulce

[There is always] the desire to do your best every chance you get. That's what will fuel me and keep me going, to know this is an opportunity that I won't have tomorrow night. And maybe tonight, I'll find the solution to that moment that for seven-and-a-half months has been troubling me.

Kathleen Chalfant

There's a moment of grace at the end of *Wit*. People always asked, "How could you die eight times a week?" I think if the play ended somewhere else, it would be much more difficult to do. I didn't realize that until I was doing it for a while.

John Shea

I find myself now, almost twenty-five years [after graduating from Yale], doing a play off-Broadway called *The Director*. We've done something like eighty-five, ninety, a hundred performances, and I'm sometimes really tired. How do you show up at night? I know how difficult it is.

We call it emotional mountain climbing to come onstage every night when you're suffering personal pain at home and your life is falling apart a little bit, yet you have the responsibility of going on in front of an audience. How do you do that? Well, what I do is I go back to my Yale craft days, and I go backstage and I do yoga.

Adam Pascal

For me, the challenge is definitely, obviously, to keep getting better with each performance. Having done long runs before, at some point that kind of fizzles and the boredom sets in. It's inevitable. It happens. So, you just have to call on what you've learned in all that time you've been doing the show up until that point. You have to call on all that experience and all that character growth that has accumulated, and you have to use that. You have to go out there and give that same performance.

Inside of you, you may not be feeling the same thing that you felt five months earlier, that same exhilaration. It's just impossible. You can't. But you use what you've learned and you use the growth of that character to give that same performance.

Frank Langella

You have to adjust yourself. You can find yourself over-yelling in a part that you don't need to. And it's only playing it, night after night, and beginning to see, *Oh, they react to this when I'm tired more interestingly than when I think I'm at my best.*

Kathleen Chalfant

One of the luxuries of playing a play for a long time, or being able to go back to it, is that every time you do go back to it, you know more not only about the play but you know whatever has happened to you in the interim, [to] inform the play.

It's wonderful to have the play so much in your mind and your muscles that there comes a time where, simply, you don't have to worry about where you're supposed to be and what you're saying. That's there and life begins to inform your work.

That's the good thing about a long run. People always ask, "Do you get bored?" Eventually, you get bored but not for a long time since life and your relationship with the audience, and what happens to the company, and the way it changes, are always informing it.

Rosemary Harris

I was going to quote Sir Laurence Olivier because he said the most important attribute an actor could have is stamina. He said, "You can have all the talent in the world, but unless you have stamina you can't survive the great roles." You cannot play Coriolanus unless you've got stamina. You can't play Othello unless you've got stamina. You can't play any of the great parts.

Richard Dreyfuss

I'm not sure I've ever talked about it in public, but it's never been my intention to repeat the performance every night. My ambition is to work and to make it different. And sometimes, you get to an edge and you say, *Oh, you can't get that different.*

8

Role Models

Cherry Jones

I'm now middle-aged and I have had some wonderful successes with things that have fit me really well. But for various and sundry reasons, when I began rehearsals for *A Moon for the Misbegotten*, I had a confidence crash. And so, I had to build a structure for this amazing role and this most remarkable play with no confidence. I had seen Colleen Dewhurst do it and it changed my life. You see, I was dealing with the ghost of Colleen.

John C. Reilly

Marlon Brando was just doing what I'm doing [in *A Streetcar Named Desire*], I assume. I never met the man but I'm in awe of him, as most actors are. But it just requires this personal commitment to the material and a real surrendering of yourself to what it is you have to do. It would be a disservice to the play to try to turn it into something different, so that it wouldn't be presented as this actor did before me. You're so far off the game if you're doing that.

Natasha Richardson

It's tough because we're taking on the classics. Whatever you do, you can be white hot and giving it your very, very best, but somebody's going to come there with their own particular baggage and say, "Well, I think you should have been like this."

I don't quite know how to put this, because I don't want to do a disservice to Marlon Brando, who's one of the greatest inspirations for us all. I think at that moment [when Brando arrived], there was some extraordinary thing that happened. This actor who reinvented the face of modern screen acting arrived.

And I don't think, even though it was a mind-bogglingly great performance, that he is the imprimatur for the Stanley that Tennessee Williams wrote at all. He is one version of it.

Tyne Daly

I've considered myself part of a sisterhood of acting. It's a great part [Mama Rose in *Gypsy*]. It can withstand the assault of a lot of different actors. It's a great part in a great play. And it used to belong to Ethel Merman, and it belonged for a while to Angela Lansbury. I borrowed it for a while. Now, it's mine for a bit.

Ian McKellen

One of my problems in playing Salieri in *Amadeus* was playing an Italian, in New York, in a British play. I went to see the original production in London with Paul Scofield and, as I thought that I might be playing the part here [in America], I'd hide my eyes every time I thought that he was going to do a bit of great acting. Actors generally signal when they are about to do something particularly marvelous. I must say that I saw very little of his performance as it was very good indeed.

Richard Thomas

I can't give Gielgud's performance in *Richard II*. But I just take as much onboard as I can, mainly, in terms of Shakespeare, just for clarity and listening to things that make things clear to me. But I like to take it all onboard. I get frustrated because then I find myself not being able to do any of those great things. Not that I'm trying to do them, those shadows and those ghosts, but they're there anywhere. They're looking. They're in the wings. They're watching. They're all around.

Nathan Lane

I myself have heard about Zero Mostel [in *The Producers*] many times now and so I don't know [if I'm] living up to it. But there's a memory of him in that role because he did the movie. All you can do is approach it [the show, the role of Max Bialystock] as if it were a brand-new show. But you don't have to go through what they went through, which is trying to figure out the construction of a show and what's working and what's not, because it's all been done for you in a sense.

Natasha Richardson

We are who we are as individuals. We're bringing ourselves to the role. But I think you can learn from prior performances. And you take from the past and then move on to now. I remember my Mum [Vanessa Redgrave] did a very, very famous Rosalind, and she listened to the recordings of Edith Evans playing the part since she knew that she'd figured out the speech patterns.

Richard Dreyfuss

I want to know how Laurence Olivier solved it, or Richard Burton, or whoever. I have spent my whole life listening to other actors and quite frankly stealing from all of them without anyone knowing it because I was internalizing it.

F. Murray Abraham

You can find yourself in the middle of a line reading that you picked up and digested some time ago, and you realize that it's not yours. It's really the damnedest feeling. You'll be so proud of this particular thing that you've accomplished, and then you'll maybe see an old, old movie, and you'll hear exactly the line reading and you'll think, *Oh God! I stole that! I hope nobody notices.*

9

Theatre vs. Film and Television

Nathan Lane

A job in a film? I'm out of here!

I'm sure I will always come back to the theatre. It's always been where I feel the most comfortable. It's nice when a movie makes a hundred million dollars and then, suddenly, they want you to make more movies. That's a great ride to be on. But at heart, I think I'm a stage actor. So I hope to be like David Burns and just finish a number and walk off into the wings and pass out.

Phylicia Rashad

I think of theatre as truth. We have this saying, "Theatre is life, film is art, and television is furniture."

Gregory Hines

I think also that it is a good thing to be able to move back and forth between film and theatre. There isn't a lot of good feeling between the people who are responsible for film, because there's always, "What do you mean you want to do a play? I'm offering you a film here." And, "What, a film? This is a great playwright, how could you?" But I think as an artist, it's really good to be able to move back and forth because the naturalistic aspect of acting on film is helped by projecting on the stage, and vice versa.

John Shea

Acting boils down to this metaphor for me. Working for film is like oil painting since every take and every gesture in every scene, every day over a period of shooting, four or five months, you can add things very quickly and you have a length of time to do that, the way in canvas, with oil paints, things set very slowly and you can change it. You can adapt it, and the portrait begins to take shape over a period of time.

In television, you have to work very quickly, and so I think of it as watercolors. The thing is set quickly and you have to make your decisions quickly about the portrait that you are painting of that character. Oftentimes, you may have a day or a scene or an hour to come up with something, and so you have to work intuitively and very quickly.

But the greatest thing about the theatre is that it is also a process that happens over time, but a much longer time than film. So, I think of it as sculpture. I think of it as a kind of carving away, out of a big block of granite. Somewhere inside this lies an ideal performance, an ideal portrait of this character that I'm trying to play. And the thing that sustains me night after night is knowing that if I keep chipping away, I'll find this ideal form somewhere within this large block of time. That's the thrill of it., chipping away and discovering.

Daniel Davis

I think it's different auditioning for theatre from auditioning for film and television, at least it is for me. There's an adjustment that you have to make. You know that you're either going to fill the stage or you're going to fill the screen, and there's a difference in your energy and your approach to doing an audition, based on the medium.

George Rose

I remember a great actor once saying, "There is no acting without an audience."

John Shea

I remember the first audition I did in front of a camera. They played it back to me and it looked like I was trying to play to Yankee Stadium. I then learned the micro-mimicry that the camera needs: the reductionism, minimalism, and internalizing.

Robert Prosky

You come to the first reading of a play and quite often you don't know the other person at all. And it's even worse in a film, when all of a sudden you have to play a love scene—I never do—with someone you just met that morning, and you have to be very passionately involved. If you've worked with an actor for five years, you know a great deal about that person and that person knows a great deal about you. It saves a lot of time.

John Lithgow

The nice thing about plays is that you are living through those three hours, the story, with the audience. They share the experience with you. When you act in a film, you have to have in your brain the sense of the arc. You have to know since it is completely out of sequence and the energy levels vary so. I've sometimes done one-and-a-half of one sentence and then, three months later, done the other half with a different background. It's incredibly difficult and you just have to keep it all in your brain.

There is a person on a movie set, the script supervisor, whose entire job is supposedly to keep track of that for you. But he or she can't keep track of the emotional life. It's all your job. It's a matter of memory. It's not what you have onstage. Onstage it has its own organic life, [the work] just grows in the course of the evening and you go with the flow. It's very hard to duplicate that.

Swoosie Kurtz

Any good actor naturally plays the size of the room without thinking about it. It's obviously very different for [the] camera.

Frank Langella

It's all changed from when I started. Now, we really are all one family. There isn't any such thing anymore as "television actor," "movie actor." You're an actor. And you're a great actor, you're a good actor, you're a bad actor. The medium doesn't matter anymore. We all cross over. There used to be this terrible division: "Oh, that's only—if you do television, you can't do film. So, if you're a theatre actor, you can't handle a camera." We're now all forced to, by economics and by the way the setup is. We're all in everything.

Richard Easton

One of the things that is wonderful now, which was not so when I started in the '50s, is that actors can wander between media. In the'50s, if you were a film actor, you did film.

And if you suddenly did a play, it was thought that your career must be on the skids.

I was sort of a classical actor in the '50s and I was trying to do television. And casting directors would say, "No, no. You're much too good for me!" And I would say, "No, that's not true. I'm not. I can do this stuff! I don't have to shout and spit. I can be real." But now, all the actors do everything.

I think there's more respect for actors as actors now than there was because it is recognized we can do all sorts of different things.

Brian Dennehy

Something can happen in that theatre. I watch it every night. I watch people, not everybody and not every night. But something can happen in the theatre that just doesn't happen in film and will never happen in film.

John C. Reilly

There's something really discombobulating about working on movies. You can get on a roll with something like, "Oh, we're doing this big scene today! It's going to take three days to do it." And at a certain point, it starts to become repetitive, like "OK, right. I feel I already gave my best to this already. We have to do that over from a different angle." And then, OK, "What are we doing tomorrow?" "You have tomorrow off." "Oh, well, shit! I was getting going, you know?"

[You have] to keep yourself ready, like a baseball player. You have these long periods of tedium where you're standing there, and then you have to run as fast as you can and catch that ball. It's a much different discipline. And I personally try to go back to the theatre as much as I can, as unprofitable as it is, because it's really like the Olympics for an actor.

Robert Prosky

In the theatre, nobody's going to leave your performance on the cutting-room floor or light you so badly—the camera won't be on the star while you're delivering a huge speech.

Daniel Massey

I worked with Michael Caine not long ago. As soon as they say, "Action!," Mike just blossoms. He just loves it.

When they say, "Action!," I'm shaking. Because it's a camera. It isn't a person. And it's also immortalized. Even if you can do a second or third take, the third take might be much worse than the first, and you're going downhill all the way. But there it is, you're on the screen. And I've never developed that spontaneity. I don't think I ever will.

But in the theatre, you don't have that you see. You have a wonderful freedom.

Marilu Henner

I had done three Broadway shows before I ever got *Taxi.* When I went into *Chicago,* years later, after having been on *Taxi* and *Evening Shade,* and even done a lot of movies, a fellow actor wrote a letter saying, "How dare they bring in a sitcom star." And I actually had had more experience than she had on Broadway.

It was so strange to me since I had thought of myself as more of a Broadway actress than a sitcom [actress]. Sometimes, you get pigeonholed that way.

Dana Ivey

There is a sense of theatre heritage and what you do and what you don't do that's, I guess, unspoken. Not that it's gospel, but it's helpful. And there are things that are useful in the theatre, necessary in the theatre, that are not good in films and television. You want to be totally spontaneous in films and television. It's the moment. But you can't just be totally spontaneous on the stage since you may wreck someone else's scene. You have to learn to do a kind of glorified, abnormal behavior that looks normal in order to feed what's necessary, because you could be splitting focus and you could be doing all kinds of things to wreck a scene if you're being totally spontaneous.

There are some things that work in one medium that don't in another, which people need to learn about.

Swoosie Kurtz

In film and television, very often you have no time for research. You just learn to make really quick choices.

Kathleen Chalfant

In movies, not only at the moment is someone else making the decisions, but in the editing room lots of decisions that you have nothing to do with are being made. So that, in a way, it's relaxing and narcissistic in a sense that theatre isn't. For that moment that you're in the movies, all attention is focused on you. But, I always feel that the actors aren't quite grownups in the movies.

Tonya Pinkins

Soap opera is the absolute most difficult medium there is, and I've worked a little bit in every single one. In soap opera you have no time, you have no direction. You have sixty pages that you have to learn in a day, and you shoot sixty-to-ninety pages in a day. So, you are constantly going on instinct. And you learn a lot of tricks.

Nathan Lane

In Los Angeles, the theatre on the entertainment food chain falls somewhere between folk dancing and accordion playing. Basically, they feel you're out of work.

Robert Prosky

Some time ago, there was a cartoon in *Equity News*. It was a group of actors coming from the East and one group of actors coming from the West, each in a convertible. They meet in the middle of the country, and they both say, "Go back!"

10

Audiences

John C. Reilly

One of the recurring, shocking things of theatre for me—
and I always forget it somehow, almost every night I forget
it—is that the crowd brings its own energy. And you walk
out thinking, *This is a whole new group of people.*

Marian Seldes

You don't see any still-life work of art, any painting, once.
Any sculpture one time. And even in films, you can see them
many times. But the playgoer rarely has that luxury, because
we cost so much.

John Cullum

When you begin to affect an audience it begins to stimulate you. And you become more centered. You become more focused. And you begin to reach inside yourself for things that you want to express more. You begin to say things that really are important to you through the material. And that's when you go beyond the material.

Cherry Jones

A woman placed a program on the stage in the middle of the second act of *A Moon for the Misbegotten*. Gabriel Byrne is in my arms on the floor, about two feet from that program. And I spent a good deal of the second act that night trying to figure out how I could politely go and kick it right into the front row. And I actually finally positioned myself where I could, I had my foot almost on it. And I thought, *One, this is going to be more distracting than the program is, but it'll be out of the way. And two, I might, you know, with a major paper cut, decapitate the poor lady who put it there.* So, I chickened out and I didn't do it. I just had to forget about it and concentrate.

Brian Dennehy

It's interesting that Arthur Miller wrote this very delicate scene at the beginning of *Death of a Salesman*, which actually has the whole play in a scene. Tells you exactly what's going to happen. And you have latecomers and the flash-lights, and the murmurings and the rustlings. And it's mad-dening because there are so many people out there who really want to watch it and listen to it.

You have to remember that they're the majority and you are playing to them. But you know, you just have to get that stuff behind you. You just have to not worry about it and just keep on going.

Heather Headley

Before the curtain goes up, I say a prayer every night. I pray for the audience, I really do. I say, *Lord, help them. Let the cell phones not ring.*

Patrick Stewart

[Have I ever broken character?] Oh yes, three or four times. And it's always been a mistake, and I've always regretted it. Once, in a small theatre like the Donmar, a girl was taking notes in the front row. She had a huge notebook and one of those jumbo pencils. This was during *The Merchant of Venice*. She was in my eye-line in the trial scene. So, I went over and I snatched this thing out of her hand and I broke the pencil. And it wrecked the evening.

Tammy Grimes

I remember one play in which members of the audience came backstage and said to Tyrone Guthrie, "The actors were going so fast we couldn't understand them." He said, "When we want you to understand them, we will slow down."

Maximilian Schell

Do you have that experience that always in the first row, somebody's sleeping? Always in the first row! I don't know why. Second row, no. Third row, no. First row! And usually, it's a man. And I understand him. The poor guy has been dragged there by his woman.

Kathleen Chalfant

I actually feel people should be patted down for cellophane before they come into the theatre.

Robert Morse

You start a show then you grow in it. And you get used to the audience. Sometimes they're receptive and sometimes they're not. But you do sort of get used to that. And you just go out there and do your work.

One night, I was out there and I noticed in the front row a beautiful woman in a Chanel suit with lovely earrings and a script in front of her. And [in *Tru*] I have to talk to the audience all the time. I look down and I see her smiling at me. And she's turning the script and I notice it is the script of the show. It is actually the white sheet script of the show. And I'm smiling at her. And she's looking at me, and she's turning [the pages] and I think, *Here is a lawyer who represents the Truman Capote estate or what have you. Or it is someone else who is going to sue Jay Presson Allen and Lewis Allen?* She is there just to bother me.

After about five minutes of it, I'm really getting a little upset. But I have to carry on. Every once in a while I look at her, and she's always turning the page. And I got to the point in the play where I looked over to her—I even talked to her—and she smiled and turned the page, undaunted. At the end of the act, I went offstage and I grabbed the stage manager—well, not literally—and said, "There's someone in the front row with a script of the play. They're going page by page."

She runs out then she comes back and says, "Bobby, we didn't tell you. The woman can't hear." I said, "Please go out and apologize if she caught anything in my manner that would have been one of those, you know, *What the hell are you doing?*" exclamations. And she was all tears. The stage manager said, "Oh, I didn't realize that at all." And they all told her not to worry.

It worked out, but that's one of the problems of being alone onstage.

Ian McKellen

In a one-man show, if you don't get the audience on your side you really are wasting your time.

Blythe Danner

A Streetcar Named Desire is very much a proscenium piece—we found out the hard way at Circle in the Square. Maria Tucci told me the other day that John [Conklin, set designer] affectionately calls it *The Wiener in the Square* because it's like a hotdog, a huge football field.

You know, after all, Blanche, Stella, and Stanley are claustrophobic and you feel like you have to be stuck in a tiny space, and that was a little difficult—[there were] so many things before you could reach the audience. So, it was quite a struggle. You had to use three times the energy that you did on a proscenium, because it's such a delicate play, an impassioned play as well. That detracted a bit, making it a little bit more difficult. But it was a challenge, and I think we got stronger as time went on.

B. D. Wong

It wasn't even just the size of the house in *M. Butterfly*, it was the relationship between the stage and the audience. Just even walking onto the stage as they were loading the set in, I realized that our relationship with the audience was just going to change beneficially. The set just looked so much more gorgeous at the Eugene O'Neill Theatre than it did at the National. I really feel that the audience is right up there, there somehow drawn into the center of that little black box with us, which I definitely didn't feel at the National.

Brian Dennehy

Ralph Richardson described acting as "the art of keeping eight hundred people from coughing."

Maximilian Schell

We have now an audience and they live with us. And when you're home, who coughs for you?

Matthew Broderick

Sometimes, the coughing is a way of saying, "I don't like this" I think.

Alfred Molina

Any actor says, "Oh, no, no, no, no!" We all have panics in some way. Forgetting your lines I think is just one manifestation of a panic. There are all kinds of other things that can happen as well. You find yourself suddenly playing a moment or playing a line, or changing the timing of something to such a radical degree that it might make someone else forget his or her lines.

No actor, I don't think, ever forgets that he or she is actually on a stage. You never get so lost that you think you're in your front room. You know there's an audience there. You know, we enter a contract. We have a deal with the audience.

Richard Easton

Audiences watch actors, not plays, anyway. Basically. Don't they?

Phylicia Rashad

There is a phenomenon going on [in *Raisin in the Sun*] at the Royale Theatre. When performers make their entrances, Audra [McDonald] first, there's always applause. And so, when you're standing backstage, you know, *Ah! Those are theatergoers! They know her well.* When Sean [Combs] makes his entrance, there's this wild scream that just goes all over creation. And you know, *Oh, those are young people.* And they're not shy. And then Sanaa [Lathan] makes her entrance as Beneatha and you hear this other amount of applause, and you say, *Filmgoers!* And then I come in, and you hear this other thing, and you say, *Oh, television watchers!*

Andrea Martin

The opening scene of *Oklahoma!* is on a huge stage at the Gershwin with just a butter churn and me coming around. I was so petrified because I knew I couldn't rely on laughs.

So, what happened after the fear of being out there? *Oh my God, how can I hide?* There is no place to hide. But what that gave me, for the first time in my life, in fifty-five years actually, was a great sense of surrender and connectedness with the other actors onstage. When you've done a lot of comedy, it's all about *What can I get?* You know, *Love me!*

Jim Dale

Obviously, the best training any young, budding comedian can have is in front of an audience. I was very lucky to have spent the very early part of my years, from the age of seventeen, in the music hall in England, touring, a different town every week. One-hundred-and fifty to two-hundred theatres over the next two or three years. That's a lot of work.

You learn such a lot. You break down that fourth wall and you make contact with an audience. It stays with you the rest of your life, so you have an easy, free-going feeling once you walk out onto that stage—also with the knowledge that you have had the training to move on that stage, to be able to do exactly what it is you are called upon to do.

John Lithgow

I had a great experience very, very early on. My very first Equity job was playing Lenny in *Of Mice and Men,* when I was twenty-three-years-old, at the McCarter Theatre, which had a high-school-kids program. I thought I was completely wonderful as Lenny, the retarded farmhand who gets shot at the end by his buddy George.

Then, I put this performance in front of kids and they laughed me off the stage. And I was completely mortified. And they jeered at me. And I had about twenty of these scheduled. I thought, "No, I can't do it."

But bit by bit I found those moments, which they found the most ridiculous, and I found just little ways to snooker it by them. And by the end of these twenty performances for kids, they didn't laugh inappropriately at anything. There were a few laughs that were just right. And by the end, these high-school kids were so captivated that they were yelling out, and you could hear them crying and saying, "Don't shoot him, George!"

It was just a matter of listening to them. The kids, they taught me.

Swoosie Kurtz

Sometimes, we'll have a night when there just aren't any laughs and you think, *Well, what's happening here?* But then, in the curtain call, you look out and see faces and they're just [wildly happy, while] all the time they've barely been [smiling]—they don't laugh out loud.

Frank Langella

We had a lot of theatre people in the audience last night. We all felt an urge to be really good, but the audience simply didn't react to us the way they always do. And you're out there thinking, *Gee, I've got a buddy out there, there's a producer out there, there's a guy who can give me a job!* And the play began to go in a direction it had rarely ever gone before. It went into a darker, sinister place.

Elaine Stritch

I think everybody has so many different ideas about audiences. And I want to tell you something, I'm very emotional about audiences. It's part of the reason I went into the theatre. I'm just nuts about the human race. And it makes me angry to hear actors talk about a good house and a bad house. It reminds me of President Kennedy's line, "Ask not what your country can do for you, but what you can do for your country." And that's the way I feel about the theatre. I think we should try every night to please them [the audience] no matter what they are or who they are. I think that they're wonderful people.

Edward Herrmann

Sometimes, they are helpful and sometimes they are an actual hindrance. We've all known it's like pushing rocks up the hill some nights. And some nights, the audience is ahead of you and they pull you, and they're great.

Mercedes Ruehl

One part of technique is just learning not to hide from the audience. Seeing the audience as a flower moves to the sun, instinctively.

Rosemary Harris

Edith Evans once was talking to a group of students and she said that when she was a young actress, she came offstage and she said, "Oh, the audience was terrible tonight." And an older actor sort of beckoned and said, "Listen, Edith, have you ever thought how good you were tonight? And don't forget, they have paid to see you. You have not paid to see them."

Tom Hulce

Whenever there's an accident, or whenever there's something that's clearly gone amiss, the audience seems to rise to the occasion, as usually does the company. And everyone has a great time. Because we've all exhibited the fact that we're fallible and that at any moment something can go wrong.

Bob Gunton

One of the thrills of doing [*Sweeney Todd*], in the configuration that we're doing it now, is that I have a very visceral sense of the audience's response, which is in turn very visceral. We share something that I've never shared on Broadway with an audience. A connection, like an intake of breath that is shared.

Faith Prince

A strong audience gives you permission.

Vanessa Redgrave

If you hear laughter, you can tell much more whether the serious things are coming off. In America, the audience is seen as much less in awe of Tennessee Williams. In England, there used to be a lot of people who would say, "Oh, I've come to see your play. But Tennessee Williams I thought would be very heavy. But what a lovely surprise. He wasn't heavy at all. It was really terrific."

In England, Tennessee Williams, amongst ordinary people, has a reputation like Shakespeare. Shakespeare, Tennessee Williams, Beethoven. And then they come and they find that here's a man writing in a way that makes your eyes and ears open. And you sit forward in your seat. And you laugh and feel human again.

Alfred Molina

My general impression, and I could be completely wrong—this is totally subjective, so don't take this to have any value at all—but my feeling is that American audiences seem to be, generally speaking, much quicker to let you know how they're feeling about what you're doing than English audiences. In my experience in America, audiences, if they love what you're doing, they really let you know. And if they don't like what you're doing, they let you know that, too. Whereas in London, for instance, very often you'll get this kind of rather polite sort of reaction. You're not quite sure whether it's happened that night or not.

Lynn Redgrave

I wouldn't mind addressing the English—American audience question. I would say, after many years of performing in America and recently returning to London to perform—and having not appeared on the stage there for many years—the thing I was again reminded of is that an American audience responds. They let you know if they like it. They really let you know if they don't like it. They cough, they maybe leave, they talk. But you know. The British audience is just like the Brits—and I can say this because I am one—it's all a fine front. The best were when the American tourists were in. We got these wonderful responses of both laughter and tears. We said, "There are Americans in tonight." I have to say, if I were given a choice of a roomful of Brits and a roomful of Americans, I'd take the American audience every time.

Brian Dennehy

The best audiences I've ever played to are in Dublin. We did *The Iceman Cometh* there, and they were the smartest.

There's a whole sequence that starts in the first act, with Jimmy Tomorrow always talking about, "I'm going to go to the laundry tomorrow. I'm going to get my suits out of the thing." And what happens, it's a repetition of a theme, and usually, by the third or fourth time he does that, the American audiences would start to laugh, getting the joke, because this guy was always talking about tomorrow, which, of course, is true. In Dublin, because of the Irish, the first time he said it, there was a scream because they knew exactly what the guy was about.

Phylicia Rashad

Sean [Combs in *A Raisin in the Sun*] said, "Know what? I've got some friends who are tough dudes, and they were sitting in the audience saying, 'Man, I had to check myself.' And I was starting to cry. I had to check myself!" That's the beauty and the power of theatre, wouldn't you say?

Alan Cumming

[In *Cabaret*,] the audience was like the other actor for me. I didn't really engage with anyone else onstage. The only people I really talked to were the audience. And they were different every night, so that made it exciting since I had a different actor almost every night to play off again. Of course, [there were also] the bits when I really did engage with them physically. That was quite scary and different every night.

Robert Prosky

[There is] the humanity that exists in the audience because, together, you build the event of performance each night. And it is unique. It is never going to happen that way again.

Rick Lyon

In *Avenue Q*, we started to become aware, through the off-Broadway run, that the size of the house sometimes worked against the laughs because people were in a small space, and they were all sitting right next to each other, and a lot of the light from the stage was splashing into the audience, and the audience was a little self-conscious. Once we moved into the Broadway house, and people were a little bit more anonymous—it was a safety-in-numbers thing—some of the laughs that we'd had at the Vineyard [Theatre] that were guaranteed were huge. And laughs that we'd never gotten at the Vineyard, ever, were now enormous.

Lily Tomlin

An audience makes you soar. That's what *The Search for Signs of Intelligent Life in the Universe* is really about—that theatrical experience of sitting in an audience and the whole symbiosis of it.

Frankly, I love the audience. It's a big element in expressing anything you're going to express onstage. You really have an absolute, genuine, complete forgiveness and acceptance and love from the audience.

Frances Sternhagen

I remember Earle Hyman, when he was in *Carmen Jones*, on the road as a young actor, and [the company] played sometimes to very small audiences. And the younger people were complaining about the size of the audience and the response. And this old actress said to Earle, "Honey, just remember, there's always somebody out there who needs you."

Anne Heche

Not only am I new to performing onstage, but I'm very new to watching theatre and going to theatre because in my life, I've worked and I was on a soap opera playing twins, working seventeen hours a day. I never saw theatre. I couldn't afford theatre. And I've just really started to go to theatre. And I am very much in awe of what's happening, and I am taken into [that] world. I experience it in full. I want an audience member to give over to whatever is happening onstage with all of us.

Bebe Neuwirth

If an audience is cold and not laughing, don't talk louder. Don't try to ram the jokes down their throats. Just be easy and gentle, and hope that they'll come to you. Sometimes, they are not going to. Sometimes they're just not going to like the piece, and there's nothing you can really do about that except just keep your integrity as much as you can and do the piece as well as you can.

Nathan Lane

For various reasons, for your ego, you want them to love you. I'm a desperately neurotic person. I come out and immediately if I am not getting unconditional love, I start—no matter how long I've been doing this—I still feel, *I'm too old and tired. I don't know if I can get through this unless they love me.*

Marian Seldes

I find audiences always responsive. I think if you have something wonderful to do, that's what makes theatre live, and people love it. Of course, if you're in a play that isn't very good, you can't expect the audience to love it.

John Vickery

The part that the audience doesn't notice actually tends to be the really precious part to you because that is the tiny little bit that you get to change every night, which you get to explore and try to improve.

Kathleen Chalfant

It's important to do curtain calls because it's ungracious not to. You go through a whole period of, *Oh, I don't believe in curtain calls or having to bow, or anything.* And it seems that's ungracious, too. So, you have to have a balance.

Swoosie Kurtz

You have to let the audience have their moment.

Matthew Broderick

I think that's the time to say it was a play in a way. That's the time for everybody, for we and the audience, to say, "We've been watching a play. Now, we're back to our life."

11

Final Illuminations

Frank Langella

You often want to be an actor because you want to belong, you want to be popular, you want to be in the center of things. And then, as you get older and you realize what a skill it is and what a craft it is, and that the worst thing you can do, really—the most overrated quality in acting—is sincerity.

Eddie Albert

Someone said, "If you want to become an actor, forget it. If you have to become an actor, go ahead."

Estelle Parsons

Acting is not a long-term thing. Don't wait for another chance: you might not get it.

Lornette McKee

People think that it's very glamorous to be on the stage and to be the actor, or the singer, or the performer. But I'm sure we can all attest to the fact that it is not a glamorous life at all. It's a life of discipline.

Rob Marshall

In a way, it's a business of "I'm sorry's." And that's the sad part of this business.

Mark Linn-Baker

There's a constant struggle to believe in yourself, to understand your own talent, believe in your talent, and to get people who hire you, and who will help to hire you, to also believe. That's always a struggle.

Nell Carter

Most of my failures are my proudest moments. Failure is so important because you get a chance to see your limitations, and you get a chance to improve. And if you have an ego, as all actors do, you will find a way to just get at it and get at it and get at it and get it. What do you do? Go out there and say, "Oh, what the hell, they don't like me? I might as well not do it." No, no, no. No, no, no!

Robert Prosky

Another thing to tell young actors. Every minute you spend, every hour you spend as a waiter is an hour you can't spend working in theatre or talking to a director, or making rounds.

Charlotte d'Amboise

About musicals, when you have to sing and you have to dance, and you have to act, it's not just preparing for the acting. It's preparing for the dancing and singing. Which means that if you're dancing a lot, you have to go to physical therapy, you have to go to dance class, you have to swim, you have to ice after the show. Then, with your voice, you can't eat this, you can't do that. It's constant preparation.

Daniel Davis

I've always felt, about being an actor, that the less people knew about me personally, the more effective my work could be. Because I could disappear.

John Shea

I'll quote Sir Laurence Olivier, who [had been] around long enough to know: "It's a subtle combination of talent and endurance." The most important thing is that if you have talent—and lots of people have talent—you have to have a drive. What it takes for somebody from outside New York to come into this terrifying city, [is] drive. Beyond drive, and beyond talent, you have to have endurance. You have to have perseverance.

Jeffrey Wright

When I was doing *Angels in America,* George Wolfe said something really fascinating to me. I was doing a scene in which I'd lose my voice. It was a certain scene that was particularly intimate, and I would lose my voice. I would get dry and I was kind of stiff.

And I said to George, "Well, you know, I'm not comfortable just yet."

And he said, "I don't want your comfort. I want your talent."

Daniel Massey

The wonderful thing about the theatre is that you can come back to do it tomorrow night. That's why I love it.

Phylicia Rashad

I think theatre can change people. Theatre can change people's lives, and if you look at those periods in human history where great changes in societies were made, you'll see that art was at the center of it, always at the center of it.

Richard Thomas

The classics are great because you feel that you've taken a great dive into this river of time. All these wonderful plays flow through it. All these fabulous actors have been in them and done them. It can be daunting, but at the same time it's fantastic to jump into that flow and to feel the ghosts and the choices. And in many plays, you find choices you've read about and things that actors have done that you know they did two-hundred years ago, which are still talked about—it's a great feeling of participation and continuity.

Cast of Participants

The following biographical sketches are, inevitably, far from complete. They are meant as a sampling of the work of the artists excerpted in this book. These notes focus almost exclusively on stage work, consistent with the theme of the Working in the Theatre series, even when an actor has acclaimed film and television credits.

F. Murray Abraham has played numerous classical roles and appeared on Broadway in *The Man in the Glass Booth, Teibele and Her Demon, The Ritz, Bad Habits, Angels in America,* and the musical *Triumph of Love.*

Edward Albee is the author of many American classics, including *Who's Afraid of Virginia Woolf?, Seascape, Tiny Alice, A Delicate Balance,* and *Three Tall Women.* He has received three Pulitzer Prizes and the Tony Award for Lifetime Achievement.

Eddie Albert appeared on Broadway in the original casts of *Brother Rat, Room Service, Miss Liberty, Say Darling,* and *The*

Boys from Syracuse, and joined the companies of *The Seven Year Itch* and *The Music Man* during their original runs.

Alan Alda, best known as Hawkeye on the television show *M*A*S*H,* also has had an extensive stage career both before and since, including *The Apple Tree, The Owl and the Pussycat, Jake's Woman, Art,* and *Glengarry Glen Ross.*

Lucie Arnaz appeared on Broadway in *They're Playing Our Song* and *Lost in Yonkers,* and toured nationally and internationally in *Seesaw, Whose Life Is It Anyway?, Social Security,* and *My One and Only.*

Chris Bauer played Harold Mitchell in the 2005 Broadway revival of *A Streetcar Named Desire.* He has appeared in plays at the Atlantic Theatre Company, Playwrights Horizons, Steppenwolf, The Goodman, and Yale Repertory Theatre.

Michel Bell has performed as a vocalist with groups as diverse as the Fifth Dimension and the Los Angeles Philharmonic. He has been seen on Broadway in *Show Boat,* directed by Harold Prince, and *The Civil War.*

Jay Binder has cast more than fifty Broadway productions including *Lost in Yonkers, The Iceman Cometh, The Lion King, Movin' Out, Who's Afraid of Virginia Woolf?,* and *Jerome Robbins' Broadway.* He is the recipient of seven Artios Awards, the highest honor in casting.

Matthew Broderick first received attention in *Torch Song Trilogy* off-Broadway, which led to the films *War Games* and *Ferris Bueller's Day Off.* He received a Tony for *Brighton Beach Memoirs* and has appeared on Broadway in *Biloxi Blues, How to Succeed in Business without Really Trying, The Producers,* and *The Odd Couple.*

Roscoe Lee Browne understudied Ossie Davis in *Purlie Victorious* before originating roles off-Broadway in *The Blacks* and *Benito Cereno*. His Broadway credits range from *Tiger, Tiger Burning Bright* and *Danton's Death* to *My One and Only* and *Two Trains Running*.

Kate Burton received Tony nominations for two shows in the 2001–2 Broadway season: *Hedda Gabler* and *The Elephant Man*. Her many stage credits include *Measure for Measure*, *Give Me Your Answer Do!*, *The Constant Wife*, *Company*, and *Some Americans Abroad*.

Diahann Carroll was the first African American actress to win a Tony Award, for the musical *No Strings*. Her other stage appearances include *House of Flowers* and *Agnes of God* on Broadway, and *Sunset Boulevard* in Los Angeles.

Nell Carter won a Tony for *Ain't Misbehavin'*, performed in *The Vagina Monologues*, and played Miss Hannigan in the 20th-anniversary revival of *Annie*. She received two Emmy nominations during her six-year stint on *Gimme a Break*.

Maxwell Caulfield appeared off-Broadway in *My Life with Reg*, *Salonika*, *Crimes and Dreams*, *Tryst*, and *Altar Boys*, and on Broadway in *An Inspector Calls* and *Once a Catholic*.

Kathleen Chalfant played the leading role in *Wit*, both off-Broadway and in the West End. Her stage credits include *Angels in America*, *M. Butterfly*, *Racing Demon*, *Twelve Dreams*. *Henry V*, and *Nine Armenians*.

Patti Cohenour appeared on Broadway in *A Light in the Piazza*, *The Mystery of Edwin Drood*, *Big River*, *Show Boat*, and *The Sound of Music*. She appeared in the NY Shakespeare Festival productions of *The Pirates of Penzance* and *La Bohème*.

Michael Crawford created the title role in Andrew Lloyd Webber's *The Phantom of the Opera,* receiving both Tony and Olivier Awards among many others. He appeared in London in *Barnum* and was seen in the films *A Funny Thing Happened on the Way to the Forum* and *Hello, Dolly!*

John Cullum won Tonys for *On the Twentieth Century* and *Shenandoah,* and also appeared on Broadway in *Camelot, 1776, The Boys in Autumn, Hamlet, All My Sons,* and *Show Boat.*

Alan Cumming won a 1998 Tony Award as the Master of Ceremonies in the revival of *Cabaret,* a role he first played at London's Donmar Warehouse. His London credits include *Romeo and Juliet, Accidental Death of an Anarchist* (Olivier Award), *Hamlet,* and *La Bête.*

Willem Dafoe has performed extensively with the ensemble The Wooster Group since becoming a member in 1977. His films include *Platoon, The Last Temptation of Christ, The English Patient,* and *Mississippi Burning.*

Jim Dale created the title role in *Barnum* (Tony Award), performed at the National Theatre and the Young Vic, where he created the title role in *Scapino,* and has appeared in New York in *Joe Egg, Comedians, Privates on Parade,* and *Me and My Girl.*

Tyne Daly has appeared on Broadway in *Rabbit Hole, The Seagull, That Summer-That Fall,* and *Gypsy.* She won four Emmys for her role as Mary Beth Lacey on *Cagney & Lacey.*

Charlotte d'Amboise has appeared on Broadway in *Chicago, Contact, Damn Yankees, Company, Carrie, Cats, Song & Dance,* and *Jerome Robbins' Broadway.*

Blythe Danner, a stalwart of the Williamstown Theater Festival for over twenty seasons, received a Tony for *Butterflies Are Free,* and has appeared on Broadway in *Follies, Betrayal,* and *A Streetcar Named Desire;* played Beatrice in *Much Ado About Nothing* in Central Park; and appeared off-Broadway in *Sylvia.*

Daniel Davis appeared on Broadway in *The Frogs, La Cage aux Folles, Wrong Mountain, The Invention of Love,* and *Amadeus.* He has appeared extensively at all of the major regional companies in the U.S. and at the Stratford Festival in Canada.

Brian Dennehy's Broadway credits include starring roles in *Death of a Salesman* and *Long Day's Journey into Night;* at the Goodman Theatre in Chicago *The Iceman Cometh, A Touch of the Poet,* and *Galileo;* and in Peter Brook's 1988 production of *The Cherry Orchard.*

Andre de Shields appeared on Broadway in the original production of *Ain't Misbehavin', The Full Monty, Play On!,* and *The Wiz.* His extensive off-Broadway credits include *Dream on Monkey Mountain* and *Harlem Nocturne.*

Richard Dreyfuss's stage credits include *Death and the Maiden* (Broadway), *Prisoner of Second Avenue* (London), *Trumbo, The Hands of Its Enemy, Joe Egg, The Normal Heart,* and *Three Hotels.* He won an Oscar for *The Goodbye Girl.*

Ann Duquesnay won a Tony for *Bring on 'Da Noise, Bring in 'Da Funk.* Her credits include *Jelly's Last Jam, The Wiz* (revival), and *Blues in the Night.* She has played Alberta Hunter *(Cookin' at the Cookery,)*, Ma Rainey *(Ma Rainey's Black Bottom,)*, and Billie Holiday *(Lady Day).*

Richard Easton has appeared on Broadway in *Noises Off, Exit the King, Henry IV, School for Scandal,* and *The Invention of*

Love, for which he received a Tony. He has been a company member at both the Stratford Festival in Canada and the Royal Shakespeare Company.

Jennifer Ehle received a Tony for her performance in the revival of *The Real Thing.* Her credits in England include *Summerfolk* (Royal National Theatre), a season with the Royal Shakespeare Company, and a tour of *Breaking the Code.* She received the BAFTA Best Actress Award for *Pride and Prejudice.*

Hallie Foote has appeared in numerous works by Horton Foote, including *The Trip to Bountiful* (Signature Theatre), *The Widow Claire* (Circle in the Square Downtown), *The Carpetbagger's Children* (Hartford Stage, Alley Theatre, Guthrie Theatre).

Elizabeth Franz created the title role in *Sister Mary Ignatius;* appeared on Broadway in Neil Simon's *Brighton Beach Memoirs* and *Broadway Bound, Uncle Vanya,* and *The Cherry Orchard;* and off-Broadway in *The Cripple of Inishmaan.*

Joel Grey won both the Tony and Oscar for his role as the Master of Ceremonies in *Cabaret.* His stage credits include *The Grand Tour, George M!, Give Me Your Answer Do!, Marco Polo Sings a Solo,* and *The Normal Heart.*

Tammy Grimes won Tonys for *Private Lives* and *The Unsinkable Molly Brown,* and her Broadway appearances include *California Suite, Tartuffe, High Spirits, Orpheus Descending,* and *42nd Street.* She appeared off-Broadway in *A Month in the Country* and *The Waltz of the Toreadors.*

Bob Gunton created roles on Broadway in *Big River, Evita, Working, Roza,* and Peter Nichols's *Passion,* and played the title role in the 1989 revival of *Sweeney Todd.*

Mark Hamill, best known as Luke Skywalker of *Star Wars* fame, appeared on Broadway in *Amadeus, Harrigan 'n' Hart, The Elephant Man, The Nerd,* and *Six Dance Lessons in Six Weeks.*

Rosemary Harris has been seen on Broadway in *A Delicate Balance, Heartbreak House, Pack of Lies, Hay Fever, Old Times,* and *The Lion in Winter,* for which she won a Tony Award. She spent six seasons with APA, and performed at the Royal National Theatre in *Uncle Vanya, Hamlet,* and *The Petition.*

Heather Headley received the Tony Award in the title role of Disney's *Aida.* She also appeared on Broadway in *The Lion King,* in Toronto in *Ragtime,* in Chicago in *Dreamgirls* and *The World Goes 'Round,* and in *Do Re Mi* for City Center's Encores!

Anne Heche has extensive film and television credits, including *Birth, Wag the Dog, Six Days Seven Nights,* and *Everwood.* She made her Broadway debut in *Proof* and returned to the stage shortly thereafter as Lily Garland in *Twentieth Century.*

Marilu Henner appeared on Broadway in *The Tale of the Allergist's Wife, Chicago, Social Security, Pal Joey, Over Here!,* and *Grease.* She was on the television series *Taxi* and *Evening Shade.*

Edward Herrmann appeared in the original Broadway productions of *Plenty* and *Moonchildren,* and in revivals of *The Philadelphia Story* and *Mrs. Warren's Profession* (Tony Award). He appeared in London in *A Walk in the Woods* and *Tom and Viv.*

Gregory Hines won a Tony for the role of Jelly Roll Morton in *Jelly's Last Jam,* for which he was also Tony nominated as a choreographer. His Broadway credits also include *Sophisticated Ladies, Comin' Uptown,* and *Eubie.*

Tom Hulce appeared on Broadway in Tennessee Williams's *A Memory of Two Mondays, Equus,* and *A Few Good Men;* off-Broadway in *The Rise and Rise of Daniel Rocket* and *Twelve Dreams;* and in London in *The Normal Heart.*

Dana Ivey created the title role in *Driving Miss Daisy* off-Broadway and has also appeared on and off Broadway in *Mrs. Warren's Profession, Henry IV, Joe Egg, Present Laughter, Quartermaine's Terms, Heartbreak House, Last Night of Bally-hoo,* and *Sunday in the Park with George.*

Judith Ivey received Tonys for her performances in *Steaming* and *Hurlyburly.* Her other Broadway credits include *Bedroom Farce, Piaf, Precious Sons, Blithe Spirit, Park Your Car in Harvard Yard,* and *Follies.*

Cherry Jones appeared in twenty-five productions at Cambridge's American Repertory Theatre before coming to New York and winning Tonys for *The Heiress* and *Doubt.* Her other New York credits include *Pride's Crossing, Our Country's Good, Imaginary Friends, A Moon for the Misbegotten,* and *The Baltimore Waltz.*

Swoosie Kurtz appeared on Broadway in *Frozen, Imaginary Friends, The House of Blue Leaves, Fifth of July,* and *Tartuffe.* She has been off-Broadway in *The Mineola Twins; The Vagina Monologues* (premiere New York cast); *Lips Together, Teeth Apart; Six Degrees of Separation;* and *Uncommon Women and Others.*

Nathan Lane made his Broadway debut in *Present Laughter,* and has gone on to leading roles in *The Odd Couple; The Pro-*

ducers; Guys and Dolls; Laughter on the 23rd Floor; Love! Valour! Compassion!; A Funny Thing Happened on the Way to the Forum; and *The Man Who Came to Dinner.*

Jessica Lange appeared on Broadway in *The Glass Menagerie* and *A Streetcar Named Desire,* and in the West End in *Streetcar* and *Long Day's Journey into Night.* She received Oscars for her performances in *Tootsie* and *Blue Sky.*

Frank Langella won a Tony for Edward Albee's *Seascape* prior to playing the title role in *Dracula.* His New York credits include *After the Fall, Passion, Fortune's Fool* (Tony Award), *Hurlyburly, The Father, The Old Glory, Benito Cereno, Cyrano de Bergerac,* and *Match.*

Linda Lavin appeared on Broadway in *The Tale of the Allergist's Wife, Gypsy, The Sisters Rosensweig, The Diary of Anne Frank,* and won the Tony for *Broadway Bound.* Her off-Broadway credits include *Death Defying Acts, Little Murders, Cakewalk,* and *The Mad Show.*

Michael Learned appeared on Broadway in *The Best Man* and *The Sisters Rosensweig,* and off-Broadway in *All Over.* She has performed extensively with the American Conservatory Theater, and her West Coast credits include *Woman in Mind, Hapgood, Picnic, A Month in the Country, Mary Stuart,* and *Looking for Normal.*

Hal Linden made his Broadway debut in *Bells Are Ringing* and his many shows include *On a Clear Day You Can See Forever, The Rothschilds, Wildcat, The Pajama Game, The Sisters Rosensweig,* and *I'm Not Rappaport.*

Mark Linn-Baker is a producing director of New York Stage and Film. His Broadway acting credits include *A Year with Frog and Toad, A Funny Thing Happened on the Way to the Forum, Laughter on the 23rd Floor,* and *Doonesbury.*

John Lithgow has appeared on Broadway regularly through his career, including such varied shows as *Dirty Rotten Scoundrels, Spokesong, Anna Christie, Beyond Therapy, The Retreat from Moscow, Requiem for a Heavyweight, The Changing Room,* and *Sweet Smell of Success,* winning Tonys for the last two.

Rick Lyon designed all of the puppets and originated the roles of Trekkie Monster and Nicky in *Avenue Q.* He has worked on such diverse projects as *Sesame Street, Men in Black, Teenage Mutant Ninja Turtles,* and *Bear in the Big Blue House.*

Audra McDonald received Tony Awards for her performances in *A Raisin in the Sun, Master Class, Ragtime,* and *Carousel.* She also appeared on Broadway in *Marie Christine.* Her solo albums include *Happy Songs, How Glory Goes,* and *Way Back to Paradise.*

Lonette McKee appeared off-Broadway in the title role in *Lady Day at Emerson's Bar and Grill* and has played Julie in two separate Broadway productions of *Show Boat,* having made her debut in *The First.* Her films include *Malcolm X, Jungle Fever, The Cotton Club,* and *Sparkle.*

Ian McKellen has played classical roles in both the UK (with the RSC and Old Vic among others) and North America, with Broadway appearances in *The Promise, Dance of Death, Acting Shakespeare, Wild Honey,* and *Amadeus* (Tony Award). He was knighted in 1989.

Kathleen Marshall won a Tony for her choreography of *Wonderful Town,* which she also directed. She directed-choreographed *The Pajama Game* and choreographed *Little Shop of Horrors;*

Follies; Seussical; Kiss Me, Kate; and *1776* on Broadway. She was artistic director of City Center's Encores! for four seasons.

Rob Marshall appeared in the musicals *Cats, Zorba, The Rink,* and *The Mystery of Edwin Drood,* and went on to choreograph *She Loves Me, Damn Yankees,* and *Victor/Victoria;* co-direct and choreograph *Cabaret;* and direct and choreograph *Little Me.*

Andrea Martin was in the original Toronto production of *Godspell,* won a Tony Award for her Broadway debut in *My Favorite Year,* and was seen on Broadway in *Fiddler on the Roof, Oklahoma!,* and *Candide.* She performed her one-woman show *Nude Nude Totally Nude* at the NY Shakespeare Festival.

Daniel Massey's London credits include *Rosmersholm, The School for Scandal,* and *The Rivals,* as well as three seasons with the National Theatre and a season with the Royal Shakespeare Company. His Broadway appearances include *Taking Sides* and *She Loves Me.*

Jefferson Mays has appeared on Broadway and around the country in his Tony Award-winning role in *I Am My Own Wife.* His extensive off-Broadway and regional credits include *Lydie Breeze, Quills, Rosencrantz and Guildenstern Are Dead,* and the title role in *Peter Pan.*

Brian Stokes Mitchell played the title role in *Man of La Mancha* on Broadway, where he has also appeared in *Kiss Me, Kate* (Tony Award); *Ragtime; King Hedley II; Kiss of the Spider Woman; Jelly's Last Jam;* and *Oh, Kay!* He has appeared in both *Do Re Mi* and *Carnival* at City Center's Encores!

Alfred Molina has been on Broadway in *Art* and *Fiddler on the Roof,* and off-Broadway in *Molly Sweeney.* Other theatre credits include the Royal National Theatre productions of *Night of the*

Iguana and *Speed the Plow; Taming of the Shrew* (RSC); *Serious* (Royal Court); and the West End *Destry Rides Again* (Donmar).

Robert Morse won Tonys for his performances in *How to Succeed in Business without Really Trying* and *Tru*. His Broadway credits also include the original production of *The Matchmaker* as well as *Say Darling; Take Me Along; Sugar;* and *So Long, 174th Street*.

Donna Murphy won Tonys in 1994 and 1996, respectively, for *Passion* and *The King and I*. Her Broadway credits include *Wonderful Town, The Mystery of Edwin Drood,* and *The Human Comedy*. She has appeared off-Broadway in *Twelve Dreams, Hello Again,* and *Song of Singapore*.

Bebe Neuwirth won Tonys for *Chicago* and *Sweet Charity,* and appeared in *Fosse, Damn Yankees,* and *A Chorus Line*. She appeared in *Kiss of the Spider Woman* in London, *Taming of the Shrew* at Williamstown, and *The Threepenny Opera* at the American Conservatory Theater.

Michael Nouri appeared on Broadway in *Victor/Victoria* and *Forty Carats*. In addition to work off-Broadway and in regional theatre, his films include *Goodbye, Columbus,* and *Flashdance*.

Jerry Orbach created the role of El Gallo in *The Fantasticks* and was in the legendary Theatre de Lys production of *The Threepenny Opera* before appearing on Broadway in *Carnival; Guys and Dolls; Annie Get Your Gun; Promises, Promises* (Tony Award); *6 Rms Riv Vu; Chicago;* and *42nd Street*.

Estelle Parsons won a Tony Award in the title role of *Miss Margarida's Way* and appeared on Broadway in *The Norman Conquests, And Miss Reardon Drinks a Little, The Pirates of*

Penzance, and *Ladies at the Alamo.* She directed several productions for the NY Shakespeare Festival and *Salome* with Al Pacino.

Adam Pascal created the roles of Radames in *Aida* and Roger in *Rent,* re-creating the latter role for the film version. He also appeared on Broadway in *Cabaret,* in the film *School of Rock,* and has recorded two solo albums.

Tonya Pinkins played the title role in *Caroline or Change* on Broadway, where other credits include *The Wild Party, Play On!, Chronicle of a Death Foretold, Jelly's Last Jam* (Tony Award), and *Merrily We Roll Along;* and *The Merry Wives of Windsor, Just Say No,* and *Little Shop of Horrors* off-Broadway.

Martha Plimpton is a member of the Steppenwolf Theatre Company, where she appeared in *Hedda Gabler* and *The Libertine.* Her other stage credits include *Boston Marriage, Runaways, Hobson's Choice,* and *subUrbia.*

Faith Prince won a Tony as Miss Adelaide in *Guys and Dolls* and her Broadway credits include *Noises Off, Bells Are Ringing, James Joyce's The Dead, Little Me, The King and I, What's Wrong with this Picture?,* and *Jerome Robbins' Broadway.*

Robert Prosky has been on Broadway in *Democracy, Glengarry Glen Ross, Moonchildren, A View from the Bridge,* and *A Walk in the Woods.* He has performed extensively with the Arena Stage in Washington, DC.

Tony Randall founded the National Actors Theatre and served as its Artistic Director. His stage credits include *The Government Inspector* and *School for Scandal* (for NAT), *The Man Who Came to Dinner, The Barretts of Wimpole Street, Caesar and Cleopatra, The Music Man,* and *The Odd Couple.*

Phylicia Rashad's stage appearances include *Into the Woods, Dreamgirls, The Wiz, Jelly's Last Jam, Blue, The Story, Gem of the Ocean,* and her Tony-winning performance in *A Raisin in the Sun.*

Lynn Redgrave made her debut at the Royal Court Theatre, was a founding member of the National Theatre, and made her Broadway debut in *Black Comedy.* Her Broadway credits include *My Fat Friend, Sweet Sue, The Constant Wife,* and her own *Shakespeare for My Father.*

Vanessa Redgrave appeared in repertory with the RSC; has played Cleopatra in *Antony and Cleopatra* five times; and has performed in plays by Wallace Shawn and Martin Sherman. She has been on Broadway in *Orpheus Descending, The Lady from the Sea,* and won a Tony for *Long Day's Journey into Night.*

John C. Reilly appeared on Broadway in *A Streetcar Named Desire* and *True West.* He was in productions at the Steppenwolf and Organic theatres in Chicago, including *The Grapes of Wrath* and *Streetcar.* In L.A., he played the title role in Eugène Ionesco's *Exit the King* at the Actors' Gang Theatre.

Natasha Richardson has been seen on Broadway in *A Streetcar Named Desire, Cabaret* (Tony Award), *Closer,* and *Anna Christie,* and in London in *A Midsummer Night's Dream, Hamlet, The Seagull, High Society,* and *The Lady from the Sea.*

George Rose won a Tony for his performance in *The Mystery of Edwin Drood,* and his many Broadway credits include *My Fat Friend, Sleuth, Canterbury Tales, Coco, Loot, A Man for All Seasons, Peter Pan, The Royal Hunt of the Sun, The Kingfisher,* and *The Pirates of Penzance.*

Daphne Rubin-Vega created the role of Mimi in *Rent* and has appeared on Broadway in *Anna in the Tropics* and *The Rocky Horror Show*, and off-Broadway in *Bernarda Alba, Fucking A*, and *Two Sisters and a Piano*.

Mercedes Ruehl received a Tony for *Lost in Yonkers* and an Oscar for *The Fisher King*. Her stage appearances include *Other People's Money, I'm Not Rappaport, The Shadow Box, The Marriage of Bette and Boon, Coming of Age in Soho, The Rose Tattoo*, and *Woman under a Glass*.

Maximilian Schell appeared on Broadway in *Judgment at Nuremberg*, having won an Oscar for his appearance in the film, as well as for *A Patriot for Me* and *Interlock*. His extensive stage roles in Europe include Everyman at the Salzburg Festival and *Resurrection Blues* in London.

John Schneider made his Broadway debut in *Grand Hotel* and toured in *Brigadoon*. He is well known from his television series *The Dukes of Hazzard* and *Smallville*.

Marian Seldes has been on Broadway in *45 Seconds from Broadway, Deathtrap, Equus, A Delicate Balance* (Tony Award), *Tiny Alice*, and *Medea*; and off-Broadway in *The Ginger Man, Isadora Duncan, Painting Churches, A Bright Room Called Day, Three Tall Women*, and *The Play about the Baby*.

John Shea played on Broadway in *Yentl, End of the World*, and *Romeo and Juliet*; in the West End in *The Normal Heart*; and off-Broadway in *The Director, How I Learned to Drive, The Dining Room, Ancestral Voices*, and *Sorrows of Stephen*.

Carole Shelley made her Broadway debut in *The Odd Couple* and won a Tony for *The Elephant Man*. Her other credits include *The Norman Conquests, Absurd Person Singular, Loot*,

Cabaret, Last Night of Ballyhoo, Noises Off, The Miser, and *Stepping Out.*

Jean Smart made her professional debut at the Oregon Shakespeare Festival, played classical roles in a number of regional theatres, and her stage appearances include *Last Summer at Bluefish Cove, Piaf, The Greeks, The End of the Day,* and the Roundabout Theatre production of *The Man Who Came to Dinner.*

Frances Sternhagen received Tonys for *The Heiress* and *The Good Doctor.* Her credits include *Morning's at Seven, Steel Magnolias, Equus, On Golden Pond, Grownups,* and *Home Front* on Broadway, and *The Exact Center of the Universe, Long Day's Journey into Night,* and *A Perfect Ganesh* off-Broadway.

Patrick Stewart appeared with the RSC in such roles as King John, Shylock, and Henry IV. He appeared in *Who's Afraid of Virginia Woolf?* at the Guthrie Theatre and in the West End, and on Broadway in *The Ride Down Mt. Morgan, The Tempest,* his one-man *A Christmas Carol,* and Peter Brook's *A Midsummer Night's Dream.*

Elaine Stritch's Broadway credits range from *Call Me Madam* to recent appearances in *A Delicate Balance, Show Boat,* and her one-woman show *Elaine Stritch at Liberty,* as well as *Company, Pal Joey, On Your Toes, Bus Stop, Sail Away,* and *Who's Afraid of Virginia Woolf?* In London, she starred in *The Gingerbread Lady* and *Small Craft Warnings.*

Tony Tanner appeared on Broadway in *Half a Sixpence* and *Sherlock Holmes,* going on to direct *Gorey Stories* and *A Taste of Honey* on Broadway; *You Can Never Tell* and *Springtime for Henry* off-Broadway; and direct and choreograph *Joseph and the Amazing Technicolor Dreamcoat* and *Something's Afoot.*

Richard Thomas has been seen on Broadway in *Democracy, A Naked Girl on the Appian Way, Fifth of July,* and *The Front Page,* and off-Broadway in *The Stendhal Syndrome, Tiny Alice,* and *Square One.* His classical roles across North America include Peer Gynt, Hamlet, Richard II, Puck, and Richard III.

Lily Tomlin made her Broadway debut in *Appearing Nitely* and subsequently created, with Jane Wagner, *The Search for Signs of Intelligent Life in the Universe.* Her film appearances include *Nine to Five, Nashville, All of Me,* and *Flirting with Disaster.*

John Vickery created the role of Scar in *The Lion King,* following Broadway appearances in *The Sisters Rosensweig, The Real Thing, Eminent Domain, Ned & Jack,* and *Macbeth.* He played the title role in *The Death of Von Richtofen as Witnessed from the Earth* at the Public Theatre.

Colm Wilkinson played Judas in the Dublin and London productions of *Jesus Christ Superstar* and created the role of the Phantom of the Opera in Andrew Lloyd Webber's workshop in Sydmonton. He created the role of Jean Valjean in *Les Misérables* in London and on Broadway, and later played the Phantom in Toronto.

B. D. Wong won a Tony Award for his Broadway debut in *M. Butterfly* and subsequently appeared in *Face Value* and *You're a Good Man, Charlie Brown.* His off-Broadway credits include *Shanghai Moon, As Thousands Cheer, A Language of Their Own,* and *The Tempest.*

Irene Worth created the role of Celia in *The Cocktail Party* in London; worked extensively with Peter Brook; performed with the Stratford Festival, the Royal Shakespeare Company, and the NY Shakespeare Festival; and won Tony Awards for *Tiny Alice, Sweet Bird of Youth,* and *Lost in Yonkers.*

Jeffrey Wright has appeared onstage in the NYSF/Public The-atre productions of *Topdog/Underdog; Bring in 'Da Noise, Bring in 'Da Funk; This Is How It Goes; Othello; Julius Caesar;* and *King Lear.* He was also in the Broadway production of *Angels in America,* for which he received a Tony Award.

Index of Names and Titles

Italicized pages reference the quoted speaker.

On the American Theatre Wing and CUNY TV

Dedicated to promoting excellence and education in theatre, the American Theatre Wing has been intertwined with American theatrical life for the better part of the last three-quarters of a century.

Creating opportunities for students, general audiences, and even those working in the field to expand their knowledge of theatre, ATW is best known for creating the premiere award for artists working on Broadway, the Antoinette Perry "Tony"® Awards. Given annually since 1947, the Tonys have evolved from a private dinner for those in the industry into a gala celebration of Broadway that is seen across America and around the world. Presented in partnership with the League of American Theatres and Producers since 1967, and broadcast annually on CBS since 1978, the Tony Awards are at once the highest recognition of achievement on Broadway and a national event that celebrates the vitality of live theatre.

Yet, the Tonys are but one of ATW's long-running programs. For nearly fifty years, ATW has made a practice of providing support to New York City not-for-profit theatre companies, as well as to students at select New York theatre schools, including secondary, college, and graduate levels through its Grants and Scholarship Program. Each year, ATW makes grants in aggregate up to fifteen percent of the organization's budget, and over the lifetime of the program ATW has distributed almost $3 million in support.

In keeping with its mission of recognizing excellence, ATW sponsors the Henry Hewes Design Awards, acknowledging achievement in design from off- and off-off Broadway, as well as on Broadway, for designs originating in the United States. Conceived in 1965, these annual awards were originally called the Maharam Awards and later known as the American Theatre Wing Design Awards, but throughout their four decades they have cast a spotlight on all aspects of theatrical design.

The "Working in the Theatre" seminars, which form the basis for this book (see the opening page), have captured more than four-hundred-and-fifty hours of oral history and insight on theatre, as the longest-running theatrical discussion series of its kind, offering sustained conversation between theatre artists.

Complementing these long-running programs, ATW has expanded into several new initiatives to broaden its reach. The year 2004 saw the debut of *Downstage Center*, a weekly theatrical interview show, produced in partnership with XM Satellite Radio. These in-depth interviews chronicle not only the current work of theatre artists, but their entire careers, in lively, free-ranging conversations.

In 2005, ATW introduced the Theatre Intern Group, a professional and social networking association of interns working on both commercial and not-for-profit theatre offices across New York City. Monthly meetings feature panels of experts exploring the opportunities available to young people entering the field, even as the meetings serve to build professional connections that will sustain the members as they advance in their careers.

The same year marked the debut of SpringboardNYC, a two-week boot camp of theatrical immersion, designed for college students and recent graduates aspiring to careers as performers. Over the course of the session, activities range from sessions on audition technique and finding an agent, to talks with prominent professionals, to advice on the financial aspects of working in the theatre and living in New York.

The American Theatre Wing maintains an archive of its media work on its Web site *www.americantheatrewing.org* where its media programs are available for free. This continually growing resource features more than three-hundred hours of audio and visual material that cannot be found anywhere else.

The current activities of the American Theatre Wing are part of a continuum of the Wing's service to the field dating back more than sixty years, when ATW was founded as part of the home-front effort to support, first, the British troops and later U.S. soldiers fighting in World War II. ATW captured the public imagination in the early years by creating the Stage Door Canteens, clubs for servicemen staffed by volunteers from the entertainment community, which grew and blossomed into branches across the U.S. and in Europe, in addition to a major motion picture and weekly radio program. When the war ended, ATW turned its attention to returning GIs by creating the American Theatre Wing Professional Theatre School, which for twenty years was a cornerstone in theatrical training. It boasted graduates such as Tony Bennett and James Earl Jones. At the same time, ATW brought theatre into hospitals and mental-healthcare facilities, as both entertainment and therapy.

From its wartime roots to its ongoing efforts to support theatre across the country, the American Theatre Wing continues to evolve in order to serve the needs of all who love theatre, whether they are students, ticket buyers, or those who create the work we all treasure.

CUNY TV, the noncommercial cable television station of The City University of New York, is the largest university television station in the United States. CUNY TV's arts, educational, and public affairs programming reflects the commitment of the university to lifelong learning for all New Yorkers. Original programs are developed through partnerships with the city's leading cultural, civic, and business communities, as well as with international cultural institutes and consulates. CUNY TV reaches approximately 1.9 million households in the five boroughs of New York on cable channel 75, and each week about one million people watch the station. Several CUNY TV series have reached national audiences through American Public Television satellite distribution to PBS stations. CUNY TV has received five New York Emmy nominations and one Emmy Award since 2002.